THE

Wilton

BOOK OF

Wedding Cakes

PUBLISHED BY WILTON ENTERPRISES, INC., WOODRIDGE, ILLINOIS 60517

Acknowledgements: all cakes designed and decorated under
the supervision of Norman Wilton.

INTERNATIONAL STANDARD BOOK NUMBER 0-912696-03-6.
COPYRIGHT 1971 BY WILTON ENTERPRISES, INC. REPRODUCTION IN WHOLE
OR PART WITHOUT PERMISSION IS PROHIBITED. PRINTED IN THE UNITED
STATES OF AMERICA. LIBRARY OF CONGRESS CATALOG CARD NUMBER: 75-175098

SECOND EDITION, SIXTH PRINTING, MAY, 1983

CONTENTS

THE LORE OF WEDDING CAKES

While the tradition of sharing a cake at weddings is thousands of years old, only in the past few centuries has the wedding cake assumed its present elaborate and architecturally-inspired form.

Throughout the ages a confection of some form has been the symbol of fertility and abundance. During the wedding banquet in ancient Greece the bride and groom jointly partook of a sesame cake in the hope of assuring a fruitful union. Today the bride, with appropriate fanfare, cuts the cake with a beribboned silver knife and the newly-married couple share the first slice together. The early Greeks did extend the ritual a bit further it is true. After the feast came the high point of the wedding, the procession to the groom's house. Once arrived, the guests showered the bride with a hail of dates, nuts, figs and other fruits—symbols of prosperity and fertility. Only many centuries later did the French pastry makers put an end to this lively sport.

To the early Romans, marriage was a serious occasion that demonstrated the almost sacred importance of the family. After the wedding vow an offering of a honey cake was made to Jupiter, part of which was eaten by the bride and groom. Following the ceremony, all the guests sat down to a banquet, very much like our custom today. During the festivities small cakes were broken over the head of the bride, each cake carrying good wishes for a fruitful marriage.

For over 1500 years patient brides were pelted by well-wishers with a varied assortment of foodstuffs! Cakes, fruit and grain were all considered acceptable, but the use of other materials was apparently common. At least one medieval city, Bologna, passed a statute in the 13th century which strictly forbade the throwing of "paper cuttings, sawdust, street sweepings and other impurities" at weddings.

Throughout the Middle Ages the wedding ceremony was to be a high-spirited occasion. Villagers were pleased at the chance to engage in riotous fun and feasting, and it was felt that a wedding provided good entertainment for all. In the hope of assuring good fortune and fertility both the bride and groom were met with a hail of small cakes on their return to the home of the bride after the religious ceremony.

In Elizabethan England the celebration associated with the exchange of marriage vows continued to be lively, frequently boisterous. Immediately after leaving the church, wine was provided to keep the guests exhilarated and a cake carried by bridesmaids in the procession was consumed with some relish on the way to the bride's home. Once home, the bride and groom, according to ancient custom, were the targets of a volley of small cakes. A few cakes, however, were put to other use. Hopeful maidens saved the little confections and later placed them under their pillows to "sleep on" and to induce pleasant dreams in which a suitor would appear. Others passed a piece of the cake through the new bride's ring as a symbol of good luck.

18th century forerunner of today's multi-tiered wedding cakes. French chefs and pastry cooks introduced the idea that the bridal cake should be a colorful showpiece to add to the grand decor.

The ceremonial wedding cake began to take on its present form in the middle of the 17th century. English royalists who had fled to France during the Puritan revolution became enamored of the confections produced by the French pastry chefs and many of these chefs were brought back to England when the exile ended. Almost immediately they set about elevating the stature of the English wedding cake. They modified the small plain cakes by building them in a shapely mound which was covered with a layer of rich icing.

Despite the fact that the French *patissiers* transformed the humble bride's cakes into a highly embellished work of architectural proportions, British traditionalists continued to break the new structures apart, brides continued to be crowned with the decorative confections and unmarried girls still picked up pieces of the cake in the hope that once eaten or tucked under their pillows they would magically induce dreams that might soon come true.

To solve the problem of such mass destruction, the practical British turned to the production of *two* cakes, one for admiring and one for breaking. Within a comparatively short time, "breaking" gave way to "cutting" and the eagerly sought-after crumbs of the bride's cake gave way to the groom's cake, a worthy innovation of the English. With the bride's cake available for admiring and eating and a groom's cake to distribute as a keepsake, guests can eat their cake and have it too!

Only in the rather recent past have most bridal gowns been white. Because of its association with "purity", white was adopted for the wedding dress in England and America during Victorian times. (The Elizabethans greatly preferred gay colors and many peoples of the world still do.)

Here at Wilton, for more than 40 years, we have been designing beautiful celebration cakes, and instructing others—housewives, bakers, caterers and chefs — how to decorate them. But our most devoted effort has been put to the joyful task of designing wedding cakes. This book brings together, in one *grand prix* collection, the loveliest wedding cakes ever, for today's brides.

Almost all of the cakes were designed especially for this book, but we have included a few classic favorites. We hope it will help you create the centerpiece for the most important celebration of your life —your wedding.

NORMAN WILTON

Royal Wedding

Your marriage day is a time for splendor, for regal dress and lavish feasting and a cake of cakes like this one! It rises to the occasion magnificently—its splashing fountain reflecting the glory of your great celebration. Serves 216.

How to fashion "Royal Wedding"

Prepare three tiers, 8″, 12″ and 16″ round and assemble as shown. To make room for the fountain, raise the 10¼″ columns by attaching them to 2″ blocks. Use 5″ Grecian pillars between two top tiers. Hang 3″ glitter bells from the 18″ plate that holds the 16″ tier and 1½″ glitter bells from the top tier. Make up large and small white roses with tube #104 and #102 and attach around fountain and at sides as shown after drying. Pipe in all leaves with tube #67. Attach small cherubs on sides of 16″ tier. Split canopy trellis in half, place over cherubs and pipe on bead trim with tube #14. Do reverse shell borders at edge of all tiers and draped garlands with star tube #15, and drop all string-work with tube #3.

8

Garland of Daisies

Bright-eyed daisies dance everywhere
on a cake that's young and fresh as
an April morning. With tall, airy columns,
frolicsome cherubs, it's lovely for young
lovers at any season. Serves 216.

How to fashion "Daisy"

Prepare three tiers, 8", 12" and 16" round and
assemble with Wilton Roman columns as shown.
Glue Wilton cherubs inside columns and make up
many, many daisies in five sizes—with tubes #101s,
101, 102, 103 and 104. For bottom borders on all
tiers, pipe shells with tube #30 and trim with zig
zag and tube #14. For top borders on all tiers, do
an up-and-down zig zag with tube #16. Pipe a
guideline for garlands with icing and tube #4 and
attach daisies as shown. (Mound a little icing first
for daisy clusters.) Attach daisies to wire inside
columns with a bit of royal icing and pipe in all
leaves with tube #67.

Tiara

A tender young look in a demure
wedding centerpiece that finds drama in
flowering side borders and filigree trim. A switch
of accent color can make it your own.
Serves 156.

How to fashion "Tiara": prepare three tiers, 6", 10" and
14" round. Assemble with filigree columns as shown,
glue lace bells within. Make up sweet peas with tube
#102. Pipe curved shell borders at bottom of two lower
tiers with tube #98. Do shell border at top of bottom
tier with tube #19, then press in filigree panels and
position clusters of sweet peas as shown. Pipe in leaves
with tube #67. Use tube #16 to do garlands and shell
borders at top of second and top tiers, and tube #3 for
stringwork. Use tube #3 again to trace vine and pipe
in leaves with tube #65.

Come live with me and be my Love,
And we will all the pleasures prove
That hills and valleys, dales and fields,
Or woods or steepy mountain yields . . .

And I will make thee beds of roses
And a thousand fragrant posies;
A cap of flowers, and a kirtle
Embroider'd all with leaves of myrtle . . .

The shepherd swains shall dance and sing
For thy delight each May morning:
If these delights thy mind may move,
Then live with me and be my Love.

CHRISTOPHER MARLOWE,
The Passionate Shepherd to His Love

Spring Morning

A LOOK ROMANTIC AS A DAY IN MAY!

To fashion "Spring Morning": prepare three tiers, 8", 12" and 16" round and assemble together with Wilton Grecian columns as shown. Make up many small pink apple blossoms with tube #101s and set aside. Trace Wilton pattern with a pencil on separator plates, then use tube #14 to outline innermost line with zig zag, then overpipe with a straight line. Overpipe again with tube #4, then #2. Use #14 to do next line going outward with a straight line, overpipe with tube #4, then #2. Do third line outward with tube #4, then #2, and outside line with #2 only. Then attach sugar filigree. Divide 8" cake sides into 8ths, 12" cake sides into 12ths, and 16" cakes sides into 16ths and pipe scallops of tiny beads all around with tube #2. Do triple puff borders at top of all tiers with tube #14. And large shell borders at base of all tiers with tube #32. Attach filigree and bells at sides and position tiny apple blossom clusters over them as shown. Pipe in leaves with tube #65 and do tiny bows with tube #2. Serves 216.

DRAMATIZE A BEAUTIFUL CAKE

with a garland of greenery, hung with Wilton filigree bells and bows! A lovely idea for decorating a reception buffet table, too...or as a backdrop for a ceremony performed at home.

How to fashion "Iridescent": assemble three tiers, 8", 12" and 18" round as shown, usng 10¼" Roman columns on a 14" plate separator set. Glue cherub figure into center of bottom separator plate and hang iridescent bells, strung on ribbons, from top. Make up roses with tube #104, petunias with tube #102 and lily nail and orange blossoms with tube #103. Do triple borders for bottom and center tiers by edging first with tube #2A, then piping over with three rows of small shells and tube #7. Do garlands on all tiers with tube #9 and top reverse shell borders for all tiers with tube #8. Do all stringwork with tube #3. Glue orange blossoms to fine cloth wire, wrap around pillars. Attach other flowers and trim as shown. Serves 246.

Iridescent

ALL THAT A WEDDING CAKE OUGHT TO BE . . .
EXTRAVAGANTLY BEAUTIFUL,
TOTALLY ELEGANT. AN EXTRA
SHIMMER OF SPLENDOR IS ADDED BY THE
IRIDESCENT BAUBLES AND BELLS.

Angelique

Baroque beauty in a cake with a distinctly formal air. The chaste simplicity of pure white is pointed up by the rich dimensional embellishments, reminiscent of Italian renaissance art. Serves 232.

How to fashion "Angelique": prepare three tiers, 8", 12" and 16" square and assemble with angel pillars as shown. Make up many sweet peas with tube #104 and set aside. Do border for bottom of 16" tier as follows: pipe out short pillars with star tube #14 and pull up to a point. Then drop a triple string border over them all the way around. At top of 16" tier, drop a single string border all around, then fill with "C" designs done with tube #14. Attach cherubs to sides of 12" tier and use star tube #14 again to pipe a tiny scroll border around them. Then attach clusters of sweetpeas between as shown. Do entire border on 8" tier with tube #4—pipe ruffle at bottom edge, then drop string border over it and another string border above it. Fill this with horizontal "C" designs. Arrange sweetpea clusters all around top edge as shown.

My heart is like a singing bird
  Whose nest is in a watered shoot;
My heart is like an apple-tree
  Whose bough is bent with thick-set fruit;
My heart is like a rainbow shell
  That paddles in a halcyon sea;
My heart is gladder than all these
  Because my love is come to me.

CHRISTINA GEORGINA ROSSETTI, A Birthday

True love's the gift which God has given
To man alone beneath the heaven . . .
It is the secret sympathy,
The silver link, the silken tie,
Which heart to heart, and mind to mind,
In body and in soul can bind.

SIR WALTER SCOTT, The Lay of the Last Minstrel

Love's Fountain

This is a cake for a very large, formal wedding—
a tower of alabaster white, sculptured with glacial blossoms. The tinkling,
splashing fountain at top is as delightfully
surprising as a bubbling brook discovered in the snow. Serves 398.

HOW TO MAKE "LOVE'S FOUNTAIN"

Prepare two tiers, 16″ round and 18″ square. Use 12″ inverted round plastic dummy for top tier and fill inside with 10″ circles so that fountain will be at proper height when placed within, and base and motor of fountain will be hidden. Assemble as shown with square filigree pillars and glue cherub figures inside. Make up roses and rosebuds with tube #104 and set aside. Edge 18″ tier with star drop border using tube #21. Do side garlands and scallops with tube #15 and drop stringwork with tube #4. Place 1¼″ sugar-coated bells between garlands. On 16″ center tier, do top shell with tube #16 and bottom shell borders with tube #32 and place sugar-coated triangles around the sides. Arrange clusters of roses and buds over them and place more small cherubs on either side as shown. Edge top and bottom of 12″ top tier with tube #19. Pipe on clusters of lily of the valley with curved tube #80. Finish with small sugar-coated birds and fountain.

Forget-me-not

A distinctive look for your wedding cake . . . achieved by dramatic dimensional patterns in icing.

How to fashion "Forget-me-not"

Prepare three tiers, 6", 10" and 14" round. Place 6" tier on 10" bevel, 10" tier on 14" bevel and 14" tier on 18" bevel. Assemble as shown with Wilton crystal-clear dividers. Make up many blue forget-me-nots with tube 101s and set aside. **For separator plate designs:** outline patterns with pencil. Complete designs as follows —with tube #14, pipe zig zag over outline, then pipe a straight line on top holding tube with "tooth" up to form a "groove" up in the icing. (Good foundation for overpiping to come.) Overpipe again with #4 and #2, then bead over with gel and #1. Next, 1/4" from outline, still following pattern, pipe a straight line with tube #14, then overpipe with #4 and #2. Then follow pattern, again 1/4" from outside, and pipe #4 and #2. Finally, pipe outside line with #2. For the scallop pattern that circles the center design, bead with tube #2, then with gel and tube #1 and then with tube #2 again. **For borders:** do all tier tops the same, except for tube size. For 6" tier, use tube #14 to do garland and fill with crescent. Overpipe with zig zag scallop, overpipe again with straight line and tube #14, then keep overpiping, first with #4, then #2 and finally with gel and tube #1. Do 10" tier same, except use tube #16 and do 14" tier the same, except use tube #18. **For bevels:** trace pattern with a pin and begin outer scallop by beading with tube #2, then bead with gel and tube #1 and bead again with tube #2. For zig zag scallop on 10" tier, do zig zag and overpipe same as separator plate design above with #14, then #4, then #2, then with #1 and gel. Repeat for other two tiers, except use tube #16 for 14" tier and tube #18 for 18" tier. Finish off bevels on all tiers with puff border and tube #14. Serves 156.

Rainbow Duet

The most inspired idea since weddings began! A big cake for the wedding day . . . a miniture replica of it to freeze for the first anniversary. What more charming way to relive a treasured moment . . . what lovelier gift to make for a favored bride and groom! Both cakes are white patterned on white, with clusters of rainbow blossoms hung everywhere. Big cake serves 156. Little cake serves 12.

How to fashion "Big Rainbow": prepare three tiers, one 6" on a 10" separator plate, one 10" on a 12" separator plate and one 14" and assemble as shown with crystal clear pillars. Make many, many drop flowers with tube #224—in 5 or 6 colors—and reserve. Trace Wilton scallop pattern—on top of separator plates with a pencil, on cakes with a toothpick and outline all in zig zag with tube #14. Use tube #14 again to do shell-and-zig zag border at bottom of all tiers (frame zig zags with shells) and to do shell borders at tops of all tiers. Mound a little frosting at tier tops and press drop flowers into clusters as shown. Pipe in leaves with tube #65. Trim ornament with flowers, also.

To fashion "Little Rainbow": prepare three tiers, 5", 6½" and 8" in Wilton miniature wedding cake pans, using a single box of cake mix. Assemble on Wilton miniature separator set with crystal-like pillars as shown. Make up many tiny drop flowers in 5 or 6 colors with tube #225 and reserve. Trace Wilton scallop pattern on sides with toothpick and on separator plates with pencil and outline all in zig zag with tube #13. Use tube #13 again to do shell-and-zig zag border at bottom of all tiers. Mound a little frosting at tier tops and press drop flowers into clusters as shown. Pipe in leaves with tube #65. Trim ornament with flowers.

Snow Princess

Snowy tiers draped with lace and sweetened with violets and roses . . . a fabulously feminine look for a young bride's celebration cake! The technique is Australian, but the appeal is universal. Serves 156.

How to fashion "Snow Princess": prepare three tiers, 6″ on 8″ separator, 10″ on 12″ separator and 14″ on 14″. Assemble with Wilton angel pillars and divide all tiers into fourths. Make up many tiny violets in assorted shades—dark to light—with tube #59, and white roses with tube #103. **For all top-of-tier borders:** trace Wilton pattern with toothpick and do free hand lace with soft icing and tube #1 to fill pattern completely—including top of separator plates. Use same tube to edge pattern with beading. **For all base-of-tier borders:** do a triple bulb border, exactly the same except for size. On 6″ tier, pipe with tube #5. On 10″ tier, use tube #6. And on 14″ tier, tube #7. Gather pieces of net approximately 2½″ wide and 18″ long. Stitch together so they form circle, and attach to cake and ornament with a bit of icing. Then add violets and roses to complete the nosegays.

WEDDING ORNAMENTS—FOR A SPECIAL TOUCH OF MAGIC

Moonlit Snow—a romantic design, with flower-massed canopy above the traditional bride and groom. Especially nice for cakes with matching floral trim—and a lasting souvenir of your most special day!

Charlemagne—reminiscent of a more elegant era, with touches of satin and glitter, ribbon and tulle. A very regal look for a large and elaborate wedding—and wedding cake. A delight to keep for the years to come.

Stardust—an ornament as graceful as a corsage with a spray of velvet orchids curved on a seed-pearl heart to make a dramatic backdrop for the bridal pair. A most impressive design, destined to be a treasured memento.

CHOOSE THE ORNAMENT FOR YOUR
WEDDING CAKE THAT BEST EXPRESSES YOU

Rose Dust—if you like a touch of glamour and sophistication. There's a special flair in the single bell-hung branch of roses and orange blossoms that curves above the bridal pair.

Moonbeam—if you're an old-fashioned girl at heart. Then the lacy heart framed with a ruffle of tulle will be just the finishing touch you're looking for!

Gracious Garden House—if you'd love to fill your world with flowers! Have lots of blossoms on your wedding cake and place this authentic little garden house at top.

HOW TO MAKE "PINK LACE":

Prepare three tiers, 8" (on a 10" separator), 12" and 16"—divide top of 8" tier into 8ths, 12" tier into 12ths, 16" tier into 16ths—marking divisions with toothpick. Assemble with swan pillars as shown and line up quarters of tiers with pillars. Make lots of lace from pattern in advance and let dry thoroughly. (Tape pattern down, cover with wax paper and trace with stiffened royal icing and tube #1.) Do side scallops on tiers with zig zag garland and tube #16.
Borders for base of all tiers: do large puff with tube #199 and overpipe with an elongated "S" scroll. Then pipe a zig zag ruffle around the base of each puff with tube #14.
Borders for tops of all tiers: do heavy crescents with tube #16 to form deep scallops around tier tops. With tube #16, pipe a zig zag scallop over each crescent, then a scroll from point to point with the curve of each scroll hiding the "tail" of the one before. Pipe beading under side scallops with tube #2 and while icing is still wet, attach reserved lace. (This means you can only do one or two scallops at a time.) Trim ornament with lace, also. Serves 216.

Hours fly, flowers die
New ways, new days
 pass by.
Love stays.

Pink Lace

Firelight

CAKES FOR A MARRIAGE IN THE MERRIEST SEASON

To fashion "Firelight": Prepare three tiers, 6", 10" and 12" round and assemble as shown with golden pillars and filigree frames. Glue swans to separator plate. Make up white roses with tube #104 and reserve. For borders on 12" tier, use large tube #4-B to pipe standing shells on side, stars at top and curved shells at bottom. Do stringwork with tube #4. Place golden scroll around base. Do small reverse shell borders on 12" tier and 10" tier and curved shell border at base of 6" tier with tube #18. Place golden-trimmed filigree triangles around 10" tier and angels in between. Place filigree contours around 6" tier. Mound icing at top of cake and place roses in a big cluster. Attach more clusters of roses as shown. Finish with golden leaves. Serves

To fashion "Noel": prepare three tiers, 8" and 12" round and 16" square. Put together with Grecian columns as shown. Make holly leaves up ahead of time with tube #67, pulling out "points" with pick. Make red berries with tube #2. Decorate cake almost entirely with tube #88. **For side details on all tiers:** use tube #88 with star side against cake and ruffle edge out and pipe with a steady zig zag motion to form scallops. **For base borders on all tiers:** use tube #88 again with star side against cake and a back-and-forth motion. Pipe a tiny shell border directly above this with tube #14. **For top borders on all tiers:** use tube #88 and move in an upside-down "E" motion. Attach sugar bells while icing is still moist. Attach holly leaves and berries to cake and ornament as shown with a bit of icing. Attach to cloth-covered wire for separator plate trim. Serves 226.

Noel

FOR A CHRISTMAS BRIDE

Something blue

OUR COVER CAKE — for the girl who wears her heart on her sleeve. As romantic a confection as ever has been created — lavished with ruffles and ribbons, roses and forget-me-nots. Serves 216.

To fashion "Something Blue":
Prepare three tiers, 8", 12" and 16", divide all into twelfths and assemble with swan pillars as shown. Make up flowers ahead of time and reserve. Do forget-me-nots with tube #101s, and three sizes of roses with tubes #102, #103, #104. **For all base borders:** pipe out a crescent between each twelfth point with tube #16 and trim about and below each crescent with tube #74—point side up and out. On 16" tier only, zig zag around trim on tray with tube #14 to define scallop. **For all top borders:** use tube #16 to pipe a crescent between each twelfth point, then pipe over sides with a zig zag scallop. Do ribbon swag on side of bottom tier with tube #127, then attach roses. Pipe in bows with tube #104 and center with forget-me-nots.

BEAUTIFUL TOPPINGS FOR YOUR WEDDING CAKE

Rose Cascade—beautifully balanced design for a formal wedding cake. With traditional wedding blossoms — roses, orange blossoms, lily of the valley.

Sophisticated — with the elegance only satin and pearls can impart! A very rich and regal look indeed, ideal for the bride who loves the luxurious.

Diamond Crown — a bit of sparkle for your cake top! Shining canopy is shaped of six iridescent Swiss tubings that arch gracefully about the bridal pair.

The Cameo

A design as quaint and delicate as precious
antique porcelain. Tiny bouquets of violets
in cameo frames give it a charming
turn-of-the-century look, so favored for
weddings today. Serves 216.

How to fashion "Cameo": prepare three tiers, 8", 12" and
16" and assemble with Wilton Grecian pillars as shown.
Glue lace bells and tulle pouff into center of separators.
Divide 8" and 12" tiers into eighths and 16" tier into sixteenths or use new Wilton side patterns for cameo frames.
Trace each oval with a toothpick and use tube #2 to
cover mark with white icing and a zig zag line. Pipe upside-
down "E's" inside and regular "E's" outside ovals. Prepare
many tiny violets with tube #59° and petunias with tube
#102 and a lily nail, and dry thoroughly before placing.
Place clusters of violets inside ovals and pipe in leaves
with tube #65. Do triple bead borders on top and base
of all tiers, exactly the same except for size. Do top tier
beads with tube #4, center tier beads with tube #5 and
bottom tier beads with tube #6. Place petunias last and
pipe in leaves with tube #68.

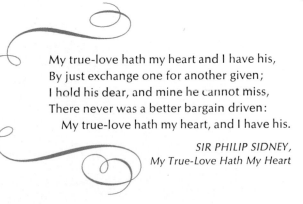

My true-love hath my heart and I have his,
By just exchange one for another given;
I hold his dear, and mine he cannot miss,
There never was a better bargain driven:
My true-love hath my heart, and I have his.

SIR PHILIP SIDNEY,
My True-Love Hath My Heart

Candlelight

Make wedding memories with candles twinkling along a pathway of pink blossoms, setting off the sculptured elegance of pure white wedding tiers. Have candles lit as you enter your reception—or let family members light them, one by one, in a little ceremony. Serves 132.

HOW TO FASHION "CANDLELIGHT"

Prepare three tiers, 6", 10" and 12" and assemble as shown with dowel rods and separator plates only. Make up many small pink drop flowers with tubes #225 and #190 and reserve. Do base borders for all tiers the same: pipe a large shell with tube #22 and circle with zig zag and tube #14. Do top borders for all tiers the same: do shells with tube #20. On bottom tier, pipe side garlands and fleur de lis swags with tube #14. On center tier, pipe side garlands with tube #14 and on top tier, pipe side scroll with tube #14. Do stringwork for all tiers with tube #2. Press Wilton steps with candles into sides of tiers as shown and attach drop flowers in a long spray from top to bottom. Pipe in leaves with tubes #65 and #67.

A Book of Verses underneath the Bough,
A Jug of Wine, a Loaf of Bread—and Thou
Beside me singing in the Wilderness—
O, Wilderness were Paradise enow!

EDWARD FITZGERALD
The Rubaiyat of Omar Khayyam

Lady
Windemere I

A CLASSIC WEDDING DESIGN

MORE POPULAR THAN EVER

TO FASHION "LADY WINDEMERE I": prepare 10 cakes—five 8" round for first level, one 18" round for second level, three 6" round for third level and one 6" round for top. Assemble as shown with swan separator set. Use dowel rods and thin masonite circles for support. **Do all borders with tube #199 and all stringwork with tube #3.** First level: shells and garlands. Second level: reverse shells and large stars with shells above. Third level: shells and inverted shells with reverse shells above. Top level: stars and shells. Trim with lily of valley and tulle. Serves 362.

TO FASHION "RUFFLED ROSE": assemble three tiers as shown — 8" tier on 10" separator plate, 12" tier on 14" plate, 16" tier on crystal cake tray. Make up pink roses in 3 sizes with tubes #102, #103, #104 and reserve. **Use tube #18 for all borders:** For tops of all tiers: pipe a zig zag garland, fill with zig zag crescent, overpipe with zig zag scallop. For base of all tiers: pipe crescents with heavy pressure, do zig zag scallops over and under. Do zig zag line around lower tier plates. Attach roses, pipe in leaves with tube #67. Serves 216.

Ruffled Rose **FOR ALL YOUNG LOVERS**

Happy Hearts

The favorite symbol of all lovers is used adroitly here in a cake that combines flowery sentiment with charm and good taste. Very young, very feminine! Serves 216.

Rambling Rose

Your kind of cake, circled with garlands of tiny wild roses. A romantic beginning for the wedding you've been planning since you were four. Serves 216.

How to fashion

Assemble three tiers, one 8", one 12" with a 10" separator set above it and one 16" with a 14" separator above it, using 5" high filigree pillars. Prepare many tiny pink drop flowers with tube #225 and reserve. For base borders on the 12" and 16" tiers, pipe large shells with #4-B and drape with stringwork, using tube #3. Do all other reverse and regular shell borders with tube #21. Use a toothpick to outline ovals and flower arches on 16" tier and sprays on top tier. Trace ovals with tiny shells and tube #14 and center with tiny lovebirds and leaves piped with tube #66. Pipe green vines with tube #3 for arches, garlands and sprays and fill with drop flowers and leaves as shown. Attach more flowers to separator trim and top ornament.

How to fashion "Happy Hearts": prepare 3 tiers, 8", 12" and 16", and divide all into eighths or use new Wilton pattern strips. Make up some roses with tube #104 and reserve. Outline all hearts with toothpick and use tube #13 to trace with icing—in zig zag on top and bottom tiers, and with tiny shells on center tier. On top tier, do zig zag scallop beneath each heart with fleur de lis at each scallop point. On center tier, do "feather scroll" with tube #13. On bottom tier pipe zig zag scallop with heavy pressure and tube #16 and overpipe with ruffle and tube #127. (Scallops make ruffle stand out.) Do shell borders for all tiers with tube #30. Attach roses, lace bells and doves as shown.

Swan Lake

Dreams are made of cakes like this—
a beautiful flowering of snow blossoms
on tiers of poetic beauty. Serves 176.

To fashion "Swan Lake": prepare three tiers, 6", 12" with 8" separator above it and 14" and assemble with swan separator set as shown. Make up several large white roses with tube #104 and reserve. Do large star borders at the base of all tiers with tube #4-B and drape with stringwork done with tube #4. Do reverse shell borders at the top of all tiers with tube #15. Pipe on Lily of the Valley sprays with tube #81, leaves with tube #67. Position roses on bottom border as shown and attach with a bit of royal icing.

ABOVE IT ALL...THE VERY WEDDING ORNAMENT YOU HAD IN MIND!

Wedding Chimes—a graceful design kept deliberately simple to harmonize with almost any wedding cake. Lattice bells are sugar-coated.

Princess—designed for a royal affair, your wedding! Traditional bride and groom are framed by an orchid garland for an especially lavish touch.

Bridal Bells—luxurious finishing touch for your cake of a lifetime! With the rich look of gleaming satin, glowing seed pearls, velvet blossoms.

Country Garden

The brilliant colors of meadow flowers are gathered against stark white for a cake that signals a return to Edwardian elegance. Serves 156.

To fashion "Country Garden": prepare three tiers—one 6" tier, one 10" tier on a 14" Wilton plastic bevel, one 14" tier on an 18" plastic bevel and a crystal cake tray. Assemble all with 10¼" tall Grecian pillars. Make up flowers and lace in advance—do daisies and jonquils with tube #104, red wild roses with tube #101, blue cornflowers with tube #14. For lace, tape Wilton pattern down, cover with wax paper and trace with icing and tube #1, overpiping for strength. Dry flowers and lace thoroughly before attaching. **For tops of all tiers:** do small triple shell with tube #14. **For sides of all tiers:** do evenly spaced rows of single shells with tube #14. On top tier, use same tube to insert side scroll design. On bottom tier, insert side Colonial scroll with tube #13. **For bevels on base of center and bottom tier:** divide into twelfths, pipe in each space—3 rows of scallops (one a "U" design with tube #1, one bead with tube #2, one rope with tube #4.) On outer edge of this, draw a three-swirl scroll in pencil and use tube #14 to trace in zig zag, then overpipe with a straight line. Attach bouquet of flowers, pipe in leaves with tube #67. Attach lace to center tier with moist icing.

BLOSSOM-DECKED ORNAMENTS FOR YOUR CAKE OF ALL CAKES

White Orchids—most precious flower of all for your special day! A very striking wedding ornament with a crown of orchids giving great glamor to the traditional wedding couple.

Wedding Bell—a perfect union of those familiar and beloved wedding symbols—heart, lace, bell and lily of the valley. Adds a note of sweet tradition to any cake.

Cherub's Delight—symbolizing the joy of love! Frolicsome cherubs, framed by flowery garlands, add an unusual and beautiful classic touch to your wedding centerpiece.

Monogram ...THE CAKE THAT'S TRULY YOURS

Something Old

AND PRETTY AS A PICTURE

To make "Monogram": assemble 3 tiers, 8" and 12" round and 16" square with Grecian columns in filigree frames. Make up sweetpeas with tubes #101 and #102 and reserve. For borders on all tiers (except base of 16"): pipe stars all around and circle a swirl around each with tube #19. For base of 16" tier, do heavy stars with tube #19 and circle under-then-over with tube #16. Outline monogram ovals in center tier with a toothpick, then trace each with a "U" and tube #16. Attach filigree, sugar-coated letters, flowers. Pipe tube #66 leaves. Serves 226.

To make "Something Old": assemble 3 tiers, 8", 12" and 16" as shown. Make up sweet peas, and rosebuds with tube #104 and drop flowers with tube #2-D and reserve. Do large borders at the base of all tiers and standing shells at the side of 16" tier with tube #4-B. Do small shells at top of center tier with tube #32. Do all stringwork with tube #5. Press plastic lattice hearts into sides of center tier and attach flower garlands and clusters as shown. Trim with satin leaves for a final flourish of color. Top with an ornament of romantic design, attach drop flowers. Serves 216.

Rose garden

Even if you didn't promise him one, he'll like this. Blushing deep pink, it will echo the accent color of your wedding (or provide a glamorous accent of its own!) Serves 216.

To fashion "Rose Garden": prepare 3 tiers, 8", 12" with 10" separator above, and 16". Assemble with cherub columns. Make up ahead—roses and rosebuds with tube #103 and latticework shutters. For shutters, draw a pointed "church window" design on cardboard, cut in half. Cover with wax paper and trace in royal icing with tube #3, overpiping for strength. Dry thoroughly. To decorate cake, first outline cloverleaf cherub frames on bottom tier with toothpick, then trace over with "e" motion and tube #16. Center 3" cherubs inside frames then pipe star border at base of tier with tube #32. Next, outline church window shapes on center tier, fill with dots and tube #16. Attach shutters, tiny birds as shown. Do all other borders in regular and reverse shells with tube #16. Attach flowers, pipe in pink vines with tube #4, leaves with tube #66.

Rose Festoon

For the bride who loves sunshine and roses . . . this wedding masterpiece, brimming over with blossoms! Tall pillars keep the look distinctly formal. Serves 246.

To fashion "Rose Festoon": assemble three tiers, 8", 12" and 18" round with 10" separator plates and 12¼" tall filigree pillars. Make up in advance—roses and rosebuds with tube #104 and reserve. **Do sides of bottom tier first:** cut circles and "church window" patterns out of paper and trace with toothpick. Then outline in reverse shell with tube #16. Use tube #19 to do bulb borders on bottom tier and shells and reverse shell borders on the tier above it. On top tier, use tube #20 to do bulb border and shell. Do draped garland on center tier with tube #9 and a circular motion. Do all stringwork with tube #3. Place roses and buds as shown and pipe lily of the valley with tube #81 and leaves with tube #66.

WEDDING ORNAMENTS... TO COMPLETE YOUR CAKE'S STORYBOOK LOOK!

Rosebud Brilliance . . . a design to fulfill any bride's wishes! Rosebud-decked Venetian dome that shelters the traditional bridal couple has an exquisitely feminine look.

Jeweled Heart . . . a dainty, demure and unusual design the sentimental bride will love. The spray of tiny velvet hearts provides an elegant and symbolic backdrop for the wedding pair.

Loving Bells . . . seem ready to peal out the glad, glad tidings. Rich satin and lace design, ideal for the bride who wants something other than the traditional wedding couple.

Love Birds CREATED ENTIRELY WITH FIGURE PIPING

To fashion, assemble three tiers with Grecian columns as shown—a six-inch tier, a ten-inch tier with 8-inch separator above and a fourteen-inch tier with 12-inch separator above. Pipe pairs of love birds with tube #10, hearts with tube #7 and giant roses with tube #127. Dry all thoroughly and reserve. Decorate sides and tops of tiers first with freehand lace—do in "e" motion with tube #2. Then attach love birds, hearts and flowers as shown. Pipe in big leaves with tube #70. Serves 156.

Love Birds ... A FLIGHT OF IMAGINATION

Lady Windemere II

CLASSIC FAVORITE

WITH A NEW LOOK

To fashion "Lady Windemere II": begin with a laced cake stand and a four-arm tier plate holder, plus four extra plates for bottom cakes. Place the four 12" laced plates into the arms of the four-arm tier plate holder. Plates revolve so it is easy to decorate and cut the 10" cakes you place on each one. Connect a pillar to center and place 14" tier on a 16" plate. Connect another pillar and place a 10" tier on a 12" plate. Finish with 6" tier on 8" plate.

Make up tiny rosebuds and small roses with tube #103 in advance and reserve. Decorate entire Lady Windemere II with tube #16 for all full and draped garlands and for most of top bulb, shell and reverse shell borders. Do all string-work with tube #3. For tops of tiers, trace Wilton pattern with a pencil and outline in "e's" with icing and tube #14. Attach flowers as shown and pipe in leaves with tube #67. Trim with angels. Serves 348.

Coronation

FOR A WEDDING OF
ROYAL PROPORTIONS

To fashion "Coronation": This cake is very large, but it can be completed with surprising speed as the borders and side details are very simple. Remember, the bottom tier and 8 small tiers around it must be decorated separately before the cake is assembled. Arrange 6″ tier on 8″ separator, 10″ tier on 12″ separator and 14″ tier on plate with 8″ tiers surrounding it. Make up pink and white daisies in 3 sizes in advance with tubes #101, #102 and #104. Pipe in gel centers, sprinkle with edible glitter and reserve. For top and bottom borders on all tiers, pipe double or triple bulb borders with tube #7. On all sides do free-hand simulated daisies with tube #1. Snap filigree arches apart at widest point, and then position as shown. Glue tulle pouffs and lacy bells to separator plates and sprinkle with more edible glitter. Serves 396.

Yellow Rose I

A cake for a big celebration, bright as all the sunshine days ahead! Festooned with flowers and frilled with frosting for a young, happy look. Serves 274.

To fashion "Yellow Rose I": assemble 4 tiers—one 6", one 10" with 8" separator plate above, one 14" with 12" plate above, and one 16"—with 3" pillars, framed in filigree. Make up roses with tube #104, rosebuds and sweet peas with tube #102 and reserve. Pipe all large borders around base of all tiers and on sides of top three tiers—standing shells, stars and garlands—with star tube #32. Do reverse shells with tube #16. Use tube #3 to drop all stringwork and garland trim, do side scallops on bottom tier and pipe in stems for sweet pea "vines". Attach flowers as shown, add leaves with #67.

Yellow Rose II

A wedding spectacular for a great gathering—lit with golden blossoms, sparkled with a splashing fountain. As lively as laughter for your brightest day! Serves 338.

To fashion "Yellow Rose II": assemble 4 tiers, 18", 14", 12" and 8" with 11½" tall filigree pillars and Wilton Kolor Flo fountain as shown. Make up lots of yellow roses with tube #104 and rosebuds with tube #103 and reserve. Do large star and garland borders at base of all tiers with tube #4-B. Pipe draped garlands at sides with tube #10. Add shells and smaller borders with tube #32. Use tube #4 to drop all stringwork and to trace stems for flower garlands. Attach roses and buds as shown and add leaves with tube #67. Finish with lacy Wilton bells and Loving Couple ornament.

The Wedding Reception

Throughout recorded history, friends and family of the betrothed pair have looked forward to the gathering and celebration after the wedding ceremony. This is as true today as it ever was. Your wedding may be as small as your immediate family . . . or as large as 500 guests, yet the observance of customs and etiquette, the sense of shared joy can be much the same.

WHERE SHALL IT BE?

A reception can happen anywhere. One of the loveliest places could be right in your own home or garden, if there is enough room for the number of guests you wish to invite. Or you may decide to have your reception away from home . . . perhaps in the social rooms of your place of worship or in a restaurant, hotel, motel, hall or country club. You may choose to engage the services of a Wedding Consultant who will handle the whole affair for you.

You can make any wedding reception simple or lavish, according to your taste and means. The number of guests, the size of your budget, and your personal preference will act as guide. Naturally, you can always contribute your own ideas in any situation, but a very large home reception is usually handled completely —and adequately—by a caterer and one at a hotel or club, by the maitre d' hotel of the establishment. So we will discuss here only the smaller home reception, which you will, for the most part, handle yourself. The number of guests, of course, will influence everything else. The average home is large enough for only about 50 guests, but if you have an unusually large home or garden, your guest list may run to a hundred or more. It is wise to keep the reception at home as small as possible for the sake of everyone's comfort and enjoyment.

HOW TO DECORATE THE EASY WAY

Keep the decorations simple. And consult a good florist. He can help you choose your color scheme and the setting for your celebration. He also knows which flowers are in season and the least expensive. You can add your ingenuity and creativity to his counsel on what is available. (If your budget is a problem, however, it is possible to rent pots of flowers or small flowering trees from a local nursery at very modest cost.)

If thou must love me, let it be for nought
Except for love's sake only. Do not say
"I love her for her smile—her look—her way
Of speaking gently—for a trick of thought
That falls in well with mine, and certes brought
A sense of pleasant ease on such a day:"—
For these things in themselves, Beloved, may
Be changed, or change for thee—and love so wrought
May be unwrought so. Neither love me for
Thine own dear pity's wiping my cheeks dry:
A creature might forget to weep, who bore
Thy comfort long, and lose thy love thereby,
But love me for love's sake, that evermore
Thou mayst love on through love's eternity.

Elizabeth Barrett Browning

THE ROOM

Flower sprays or branches of foliage can be the main decoration for your reception room. One or more elaborate arrangements can be used on the reception table and a small arrangement of the same color on each smaller table, if you plan to use them. Use color with care . . . the favorite choice is traditional white with a single accent color, perhaps taken from the color of the bridesmaids' gowns.

If you have a pretty garden and the weather is fine, there is nothing quite as delightful as a garden wedding. Nature then provides most of the decorations, and of course you can add your share. However, be ready to move the party indoors in case of rain.

Add something unusual to your reception decor . . . for a touch that will always be remembered. Wilton's miniature pottery pieces are authentic replicas of treasured heirlooms, hand-made and hand-painted in Italy. Some are embellished with sculptured flowers, all are tiny works of art! Marvelous take-home mementos!

THE ALTAR

If your ceremony is also to be held at home, pick a natural spot, in front of a fireplace, perhaps . . . or mass greenery in any corner. In a garden, you might use a trellis or a lovely rosebush for a backdrop. A white cloth runner or flower-trimmed posts can form an aisle. Incidently, satin ribbon can be used as an inexpensive substitute for flowers in many cases. (Your florist will handle the placing of ribbons and runner as well as flowers, if you wish.)

THE RECEPTION TABLE

The most natural idea is to let the wedding cake be the focal point . . . centering the reception table or on a separate table of its own. This beautiful and time-honored confection is really the most essential decoration of all. With it, little else is needed. You and your baker can pick from any of the wedding cake designs in this book, changing the color scheme to suit your individual taste. He will advise you on which would be the most suitable for your reception. Or, of course, you or one of your friends may decide to make the wedding cake yourself. This book gives all the directions you need and nothing could be a lovelier gift to the bride!

THE ACCESSORIES

You can also have, as objects of decor, monogrammed matches, petits fours with the names or initials of the bride and groom and personalized napkins. Or put together your own imaginative decorations . . . see the attractive Wilton suggestions throughout this book. Some of the decorations can also serve as momentos of the occasion for guests to take home with them.

THE FLOWERS

Flowers have been an important part of wedding ceremonies and celebrations from ancient times. Roman brides wore bunches of sweet scented herbs under their veils and carried sheaves of wheat to symbolize the hoped-for life of plenty. And later the Saracens carried orange blossoms as a symbol of fertility. You can use the lovely symbolism of flowers at your reception, keeping in mind of course, the seasonal availability. To help you choose:

Flowers of the month and birth flowers:

January—Carnations
February—Primroses
March—Violets
April—Daisies
May—Lily of the Valley
June—Roses
July—Larkspur
August—Poppy
September—Morning Glory
October—Cosmos
November—Chrysanthemums
December—Holly

What the flowers say:
Carnations—white, true love
        pink, remembrance
Daisies—discretion, honesty
Roses—red, love; white, innocence
Gladiolas—sincerity
Chrysanthemums—truth, hope, friendship
Camellias—red, passion
        white, loveliness; pink, longing
Forget Me Not—remembrance
Narcissus—sweet nature
Stephanotis—I will follow my love
Violets—true love
Lily of the Valley—fulfillment
Sweet Peas—gratitude
Asters—charm
Gardenias—secret love
Lily—happiness
Orange blossom—purity and loveliness
Orchid—you are beautiful

Serene swans make a beautiful starting point for a bridal table floral arrangement.
Just one of the many Wilton ways to do your own reception decorations.

HOW TO SERVE YOUR GUESTS

For a guest-list of twenty or less, a sit-down meal will probably be the best choice. In this case, the reception and bride's table will be one and the wedding cake can be the main decoration (although it is better to have it at one end rather than at center, for more comfortable serving and conversation.)

If you have more than twenty guests, a buffet table is the best solution. The wedding party—bride, groom, parents and attendants—should still have a table available, but they may prefer to circulate among the guests. Bride and groom sit in center of bride's table, maid of honor at groom's left, best man at bride's right. The other attendants sit on either side, men and women alternating when possible.

Elegant new way for guests to serve themselves! Wilton's beverage fountain dispenses punch or champagne in three gently flowing arcs. (A hidden electric pump does the work.)

In earliest times, "evil spirits" were frightened away from happy ceremonials by loud, clanging noises, the beating of drums or the blowing of horns. (We see an echo of this today in our New Year celebrations). Gradually, the sweet sounds of music replaced the din for the marriage celebration and to this day, music is a very important part of both ceremony and reception.

HOW TO SERENADE THEM

Your music can be as simple as a strolling accordianist or pianist or as elaborate as a small band. For a home wedding, recordings can provide perfectly suitable music. But do try to have some kind of music —it is one of the oldest traditions of the wedding celebration. If you have room for dancing, so much the better. It will add great joy to the whole occasion.

To add an air of elegance to even the smallest reception, use the finest possible china, crystal and silver serving dishes and candelabra. If the bride's mother cannot supply them, it is worth considering borrowing or renting them. If you do not have enough china and silver in one pattern, more than one may be used. In fact, some hostesses use more than one pattern deliberately to add interest to the table.

HOW TO KEEP THE TRADITIONS

The reception line—a formal lining-up is only necessary where there are more than 25 guests. As guests enter the reception room, they are greeted by the bride's mother, the groom's mother, the bride and groom and the maid of honor. The fathers of the bride and groom and the other members of the wedding party can also participate, but it is not required.

The wedding toast—at a buffet, guests can be served punch, wine or champagne as soon as they have passed through the reception line. At a sit-down dinner, the bride's glass is filled first, then the groom's and after that all the attendants, beginning with the maid of honor. As soon as everyone is served, the best man rises and makes the first toast. Or at a buffet, he asks for everyone's attention and then makes the toast.

The cake-cutting ceremony—at a sit-down meal, the cake is cut just before dessert and served with ice cream or fruit ices. At a buffet, it is cut just before the bride and groom leave. The bride cuts the first slice with her husband's hand over hers. They share the first taste and then someone else takes over to serve the rest of the guests. If the groom is in military service, he may wish to use a sword or saber to cut the cake.

The tossing of the bouquet—just before she leaves the reception to change into her going-away clothes, the bride tosses her wedding bouquet to her bridesmaids and the single girl guests. The one who catches the bouquet, so legend says, will marry next.

The tossing of the garter—after throwing the bouquet, some brides also toss a garter to the ushers and other single men at the reception. Sometimes the groom removes the garter (placed below the knee) and the bride tosses it over her shoulder as she did the bouquet. Again, the man who catches it is supposed to be next to marry.

The shower of rice—the bride and groom appear in their going-away clothes and guests shower them with rice as they leave. This is a custom that goes back to ancient times, expressing a wish for prosperity and fertility. Little bags of rice can be distributed to guests or placed in pretty containers on the reception table. Recently, real or paper roses are being substituted for rice. The choice is up to you.

Give all to love:
  Obey thy Heart;
Friends, kindred, days,
Estate, good fare,
Plans, credit and the Muse,—
Nothing refuse
  RALPH WALDO EMERSON   Give All to Love

Down on your knees, And thank Heaven, fasting, for a good man's love.
  WILLIAM SHAKESPEARE   As You Like It

60

HOW TO SAVE THE DAY

Take pictures. Photographs taken at your wedding and reception are among the most important of your life. They'll be the pictures you and your family will treasure always and the ones you'll show to your children. For this reason, it is wise to consider hiring a professional photographer, for even if you have a friend or relative who is willing to take the pictures, he may lack the skill or experience to "tell the story" properly. Be sure you know what the cost will be ahead of time, and make an early reservation, especially if you are marrying in a popular month such as June.

WHAT TO SERVE YOUR GUESTS

If you are having a buffet, a perfectly appropriate and very pretty home reception can be as simple as this: wedding cake centerpiece, champagne or fruit punch bowl, tiny finger sandwiches and canapes, nuts, mints and coffee. If you wish to add more food to your buffet, or if you are serving a sit-down meal, let the time of day be your guide. A morning or early afternoon reception is called a "breakfast" and you can offer traditional breakfast or brunch dishes. Late afternoon or evening dishes can be heartier and more elaborate. But remember, when making buffet food choices, that guests may have to stand and hold their plates while they eat . . . so choose dishes that can be eaten easily and with a fork only.

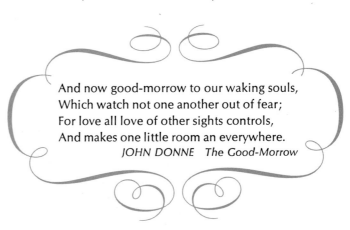

And now good-morrow to our waking souls,
Which watch not one another out of fear;
For love all love of other sights controls,
And makes one little room an everywhere.
JOHN DONNE   The Good-Morrow

Lace Fantasy

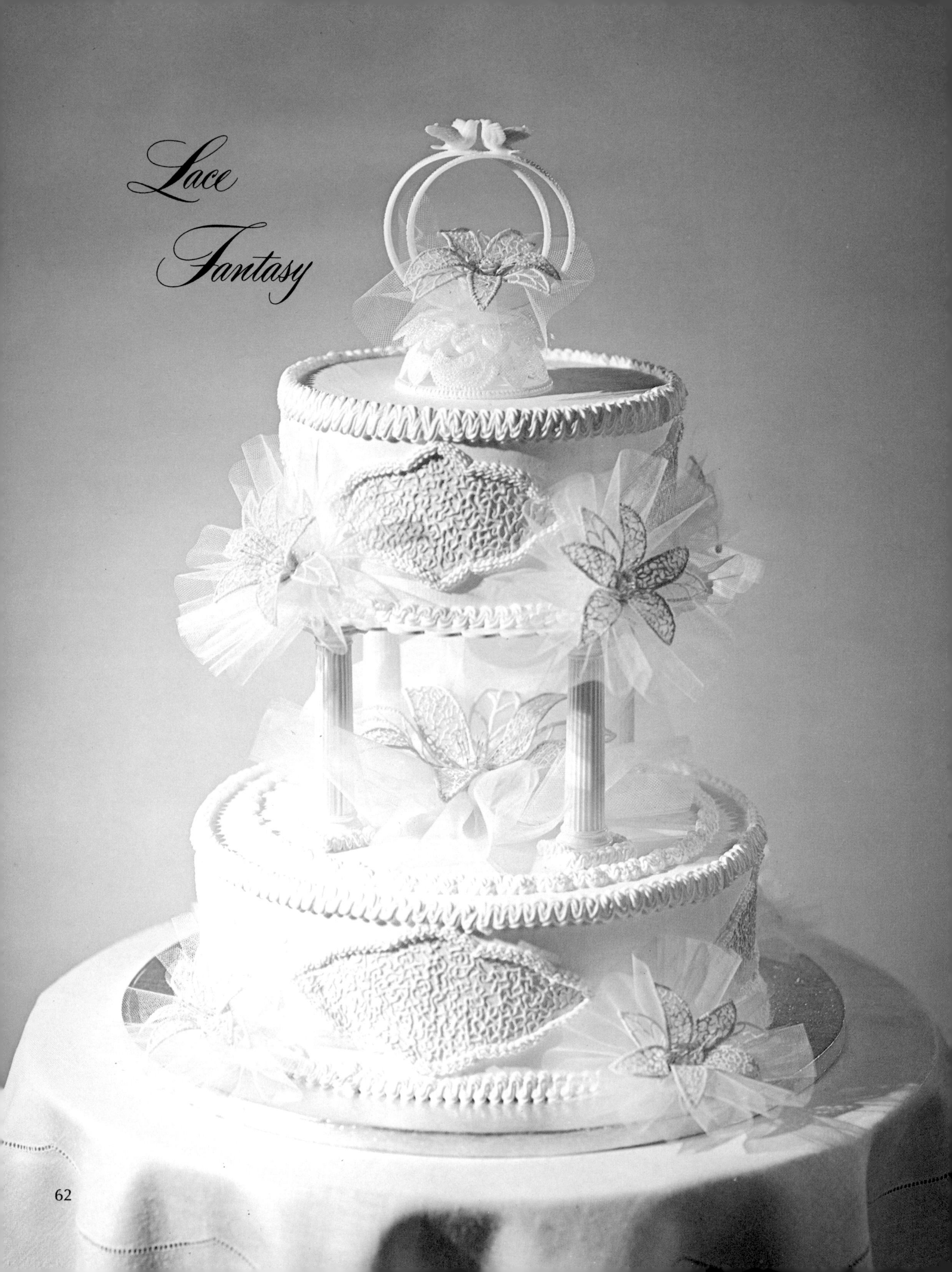

Petite Wedding Cakes

Even if your wedding is so small and intimate that only the immediate family is present, you can have a true and beautiful . . . wedding cake. In the designs that follow, you'll see the lavish details, the festive flair of the most elaborate cakes, translated into mini-masterpieces that serve as few as thirty guests.

HOW TO MAKE "LACE FANTASY" CAKE

Assemble two tiers, one 8" and one 12" round with classic columns in between. Frost both in white buttercream and pipe top and bottom zig-zag borders of each tier and an inner circle on top of lower tier with tube #16. Gather net for "frou-frous" and attach with a bit of icing as shown. To make net flowers and leaves, place Wilton patterns on stiff net or tulle and cut out. Attach each net petal and leaf to curved Wilton flower form and use tube #1 to pipe free-hand lace within petals. Then use same tube to outline petals and leaves, overpiping for strength. Let remain on curved form until completely dry. Put flowers and leaves together in center of frou-frous with dab of wet icing. Do side medallions by tracing pattern on cake, outline with zig zag and tube #14 and pipe free-hand lace inside with tube #1. Serves 98.

Heart of Flowers

To make "Heart of Flowers": assemble a two-layer cake baked in Wilton heart-shaped pan and a three-layer cake 14" square. For top border of heart, pipe large puffs with tube #199, overpipe pink "C" scrolls and surround with zig zag scallops, both done with tube #14. Do similar border for bottom of heart, but make scroll longer and do zig zag scallops with tube #16. Use tube #199 again to pipe "posts" up sides of square and do crescents in between. Use tube #14 to do more long pink scrolls. Pipe a zig zag border around base of cake. Do all string-work with tube #3. Pipe flowers ahead of time, using tube #101s for forget-me-nots, #104 for daisies and roses and position as shown. Pipe in leaves with tube #65 and #67. Serves 102.

Bride's Rainbow

Delightful design for
the bride who wants a
rainbow color scheme.

To make "Bride's Rainbow": prepare two tiers, 6" and 10" round and assemble with angel columns as shown. Make up tiny drop flowers with tube #225 in assorted pastel colors—pink, yellow, blue, green and violet. Arrange on cake as shown and attach to fine florist's wire to tuck into tulle trimmed inverted lace bell in center of separator. (Attach also to top ornament.) Pipe top and bottom shell border on both tiers with tube #30. Do ribbon ruffle scallops around large tier with tube #104. Swirl colonial scroll around sides of top tier with tube #104, trim shells at base of both tiers and ribbon ruffles with tube #14. Do all stringwork with tube #2. Serves 64.

GLAMOROUS ORNAMENTS—SCALED TO PETITE CAKES

Double Ring Ceremony — designed with great simplicity to symbolize your exchange of rings and love. Complete with turtle doves and pearlized wedding rings, it will serve as a treasured memento of your day of days for many years to come.

Triple Bells — gladsome bells for the top of your wedding cake, swinging out from a dainty filigree heart base to ring out the joyous wedding day news. Versatile sugar-frosted lace design will add an elegant touch to just about any petite cake.

Dainty Charm—a very lovely little ornament certain to give your petite wedding cake an important extra touch of beauty. Traditional bridal couple is set off by a breathtaking backdrop of orange blossoms and gossamer tulle.

HOW TO MAKE THE "LACE WHEEL"

This is not an easy cake to do, but it will be easier if you are careful to do it in steps *exactly* as described below. *Step 1:* make many tiny forget-me-nots with tube #101s and dry for later use. *Step 2:* tape down Wilton filigree bevel pattern and cover with wax paper. Then trace pattern with Color Flow icing and tube #1. Dry on a piece of curved styrofoam so bevels will be shaped correctly. Overpipe again to make bevels firmer and while this second layer of icing is still wet, sprinkle with white edible glitter and attach little forget-me-nots to form heart shapes with a little royal icing. Pipe in leaves with tube #65 and allow all to dry thoroughly. *Step 3:* assemble a one-layer cake, 8" round and 1" high and a two-layer cake, 12" round on a 16" round piece of heavy cardboard. Ice all (including cardboard) in white buttercream. Divide cake edges and board edge evenly into twelfths—and divide side of 12" cake into twelfths marked one-inch up from base. Then add side details.
Use tube #1 to pipe two rows of yellow "U's" in scallop

effect as shown. With tube #2, add a frame of white beading around the "U's". Finally, do more beading around cake bases with tube #4. *Step 4:* do green stem lines on top of 8" cake between twelfth marks as shown. Attach Forget-Me-Nots in a floral spray and along stems and pipe leaves on stems, also. Attach single blossoms to side design, as shown. *Step 5:* pipe a line of soft icing between one section of twelfth marks at top edge of 8" cake and top edge of 12" cake. Then attach your first filigree bevel, being very careful as it is very fragile. Repeat soft icing and filigree, one bevel at a time, until entire top is complete. *Step 6:* pipe triple bead border with tube #2 all around tops of 8" and 12" cakes, to conceal where filigree meets cake edges. *Step 7:* repeat filigree technique for 12" cake, piping soft icing one section at a time on line at side of cake and on edge of board, then adding filigree. When complete, again pipe beading with tube #3 to conceal where filigree joins. Finish with double row of beading around board edge.

Lace Wheel...A DECORATOR'S MASTERPIECE!

For your small but elegant wedding reception, this work of art in icing—
a design much in the fabled Lambeth style. Lush Venise lace—done in icing—
circles to form an exquisite three-dimensional
frame for a two-tiered cake that will serve 68.

Champagne honeymoon

A toast to the happy couple, made a pretty part of their wedding centerpiece! The design has a feeling of old-world elegance and the impressive architecture of a much larger cake. Wedding splendor scaled down to serve 66 guests.

HOW TO FASHION "CHAMPAGNE HONEYMOON"

Prepare two tiers, one 6" round and one 10" square. Place 6" round cake on an 8" separator plate and assemble all together with Grecian columns as shown. Make up wild roses with tube #102. For top border of round cake, use tube #16 to pipe a garland, curve a zig zag crescent under it and top it with small shells. Do a fleur de lis between each scallop, also with tube #16. For base of round cake, pipe a shell border with tube #30. On square cake, do top, separator plate and base border with same. For Viennese style side detail, make a standing scroll and do a zig zag inside it with star tube #16. Attach flowers as shown, pipe in leaves with tube #67 and decorate with small sugar-frosted bells and miniature champagne glasses. Just before the cake-cutting ceremony, fill with champagne.

WEDDING ORNAMENTS...THE CROWNING TOUCH FOR YOUR LOVELY CAKE

Petite Floral Fantasy — especially sized for petite cakes. Yet so dramatic is the flourish of flowers and leaves curved around the bridal couple, that it seems much larger. A charming keepsake for the years to come.

Morning Rosebud — with a lovely touch of symbolism. Bride and groom stand before an open garden gate ready to step into a new life together. Delicate filigree adds a pretty touch to any wedding cake design.

Petite Dainty Charm — an especially lovely ornament, designed to give the smaller wedding cake an extra touch of beauty and importance. The traditional bridal couple is set off by a backdrop of orange blossoms and gossamer tulle.

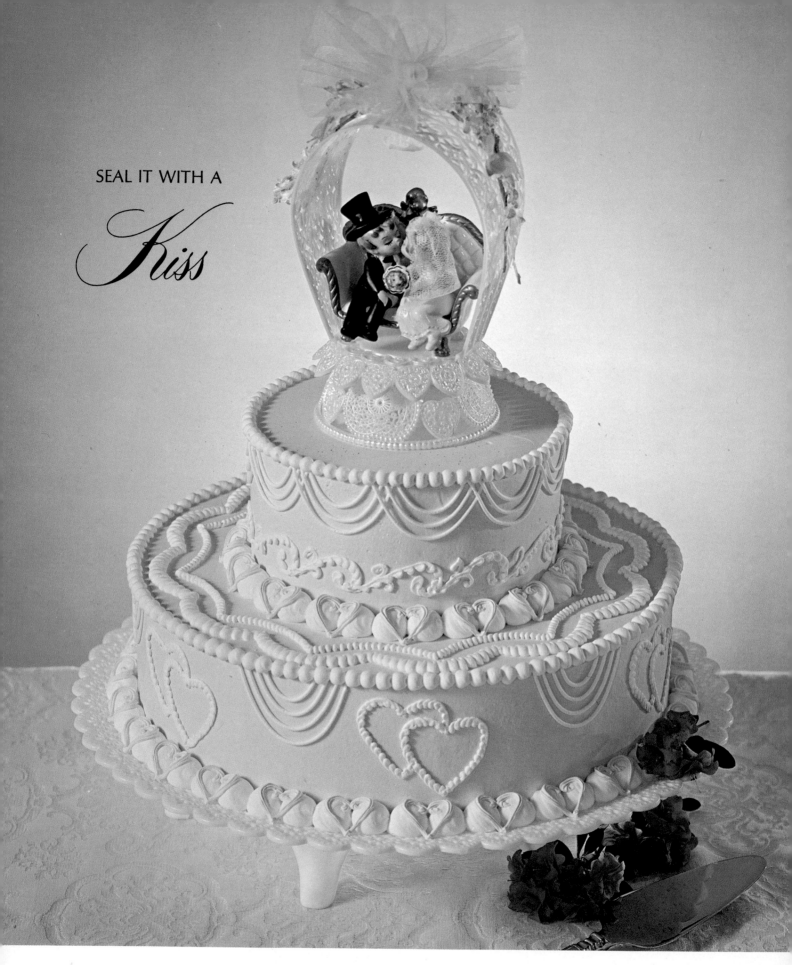

SEAL IT WITH A

Kiss

WHIMSICAL CHARM...OUR PETITE "LOVING COUPLE" CAKE

Pink Daisy

Daisies do tell a story of love and beauty. They're scattered everywhere, even on the fetching froth of tulle above the tiny bride and groom. Serves 114.

To make Pink Daisy: prepare three tiers, 6", 8" and 12" round. Then make a laced cake stand for a petite cake by using 8", 10" and 14" size Wilton plates and gluing six Wilton legs to bottom plate. Make pink daisies in advance with royal icing and tubes 101s, 101 and 102. Do centers with pink piping jel and sprinkle all flowers with edible glitter. Do the same borders and details on all three tiers. First, divide each tier evenly into 12 sections, marking them off with a toothpick. Then outline scallop design on tops of tiers and use tube #2 to trace scallops with white beading. Next pipe "U" design with pink piping jel. Start with a zig-zag motion, forming scallop on cake sides from twelfth mark to twelfth mark. Then fill in scallops with a full garland. Pipe a zig-zag scallop over the garland, starting at scallop points, going in from point and out over garland, then in again to point. Make shells at base of tiers with tube #30. Do all pink stringwork on scallops and shells with tube #2. Add delicate green stemwork with tube #2 and do leaves with tube #67. Attach daisies with dot of icing to cake and top ornament.

To make "Loving Couple" cake: prepare two tiers, one 8" and one 12" round. Use Wilton pattern for top of 12" tier. Trace pattern with icing and do a "rope" of dots with tube #3 for inside scallop line. Do zig-zag with tube #4 for outside scallop lines. Pipe small bulb borders at cake tops with tube #6 and large bulb borders at base of cakes with tube #10. Pipe pink hearts over larger bulbs with tube #14. Do stringwork, colonial scroll and tiny heart borders with tube #2. Serves 98.

SOMETHING NEW

For today's bride and groom, this nouveau-art cake. The colors are clear and strong, the shape clean and linear, the mood mod. Serves 100.

To make "Something New" cake: prepare three tiers, 6", 8" and 10" square and frost in bright colors (yellow, shocking pink and orange) *before* assembling. Make up large drop flowers with tube #1F, medium drop flowers with tube #2F and centers for both with tube #4.

Draw hearts on sides of cakes with toothpick and outline with zig zag and tube #14. Pipe bottom tier shell border with tube #32, middle with tube #19 and top with tube #16. Mound frosting on top to hold candle and push flowers in all around. Attach rest of flowers as shown.

THE WEDDING CAKE OF YOUR DREAMS CAN BE YOURS

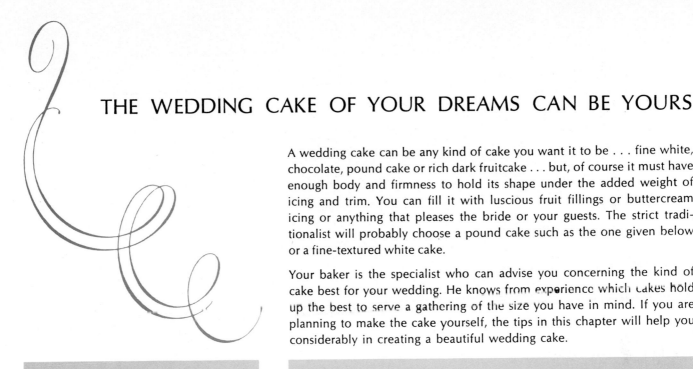

A wedding cake can be any kind of cake you want it to be . . . fine white, chocolate, pound cake or rich dark fruitcake . . . but, of course it must have enough body and firmness to hold its shape under the added weight of icing and trim. You can fill it with luscious fruit fillings or buttercream icing or anything that pleases the bride or your guests. The strict traditionalist will probably choose a pound cake such as the one given below or a fine-textured white cake.

Your baker is the specialist who can advise you concerning the kind of cake best for your wedding. He knows from experience which cakes hold up the best to serve a gathering of the size you have in mind. If you are planning to make the cake yourself, the tips in this chapter will help you considerably in creating a beautiful wedding cake.

Groom's Fruitcake

3 cups flour
2 teaspoons baking soda
1 teaspoon baking powder
½ teaspoon ground cloves
½ teaspoon nutmeg
½ teaspoon cinnamon
½ teaspoon salt
1 pound candied cherries
½ pound mixed candied fruit
½ pound candied pineapple
¾ cup dates
1 cup raisins
1½ cups pecans
1½ cups walnuts
½ cup butter
1 cup sugar
2 eggs
½ cup grape juice
1½ cups applesauce

Sift and mix flour, baking soda, baking powder, spices and salt. Cut up fruit and coarsely chop nuts. Mix fruit and nuts. Cream butter and sugar. Add eggs and beat well. Beating until blended after each addition, alternately add dry ingredients and grape juice to creamed mixture. Mix in fruit, nuts and applesauce. Turn into a greased 11" ring pan or 10" tube pan. Bake at 275°F about 2¼ hours. Run a knife around tube and sides and let set about 10 minutes in pan. Remove cake from pan and cool thoroughly. Recipe yields one six pound fruitcake.

Wedding Pound Cake

4 cups sifted flour
2 teaspoons baking powder
1 teaspoon salt
½ teaspoon ground mace
2 cups butter
1 tablespoon vanilla
2¼ cups sugar
8 large eggs
½ cup milk

Grease and flour desired pans (see chart below). Sift together flour, baking powder, salt and mace; set aside. Cream butter with vanilla until softened. Gradually add sugar, beating until fluffy. Add eggs, one at a time, beating thoroughly after each addition, until mixture is light and fluffy. Add dry ingredients alternately in thirds with the milk in halves to creamed mixture, mixing only until smooth after each addition. Fill pans with batter as indicated. Repeat recipe as needed for amount of batter to fill pans. Bake at 300°F for the time indicated. Cool in pans on wire racks ten minutes for 6" and 8" pans and 20 minutes for 12" pans. Turn out of pans and cool thoroughly. About 9¼ cups batter.

PANS (2" DEEP)	AMOUNT OF BATTER	BAKING TIME
6" round	1¾ to 2 cups	40 to 50 minutes
8" round	3½ to 4 cups	55 to 60 minutes
12" round	8 cups	1 hour

GROOM'S CAKE

This is the second cake that is often packaged for guests to take home and "dream upon". It is a charming custom with an interesting history (for its origin, see "The Lore of Wedding Cakes", page 3) and one you may want at your wedding.

Groom's cake is usually rich fruitcake or sometimes a devil's food cake. It is cut into small pieces and put into tiny beribboned boxes or envelopes. These are arranged on a table so guests can help themselves.

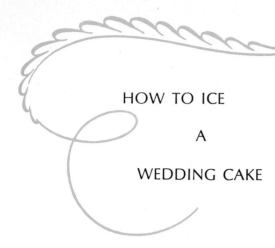

HOW TO ICE

A

WEDDING CAKE

It is icing that can make all the difference in the beauty and flavor of this grandest of all celebration cakes. A rich icing outside and a creamy filling within will also keep the cake moist and delicious, a treat for the palate as well as the eye. Finally, not the least of icing's functions is to hold the many layers together smoothly. We've given four basic icing recipes: buttercream and boiled icings for frosting the cake and for piping borders, stringwork and leaves. And royal icing for making lifelike frosting flowers that never wilt.

ICING AND FILLING THE CAKE

Cool layers thoroughly on cake racks after baking, then brush off loose crumbs. Refrigerate or freeze for at least a day before decorating, so layers will be firm enough to hold their shape and handle easily. Use the best ingredients, so the cake will stay fresh and delicious.

When cake is ready, secure one layer to a cardboard cake circle the same size as layer. Place on turntable or tray. Spread icing with a spatula on top of base layer to about ¼″ from edge. Add top layer upside down on first. Brush crumbs from cake. Then brush with apricot glaze (heat one cup apricot jam to boiling and strain). Let dry until crust forms to seal in any other crumbs and to add a delicious flavor.

Frost sides of cake first. Using a long spatula, spread plenty of icing on side, building edges up slightly higher than cake. Use long, even strokes, working from the bottom up. Then cover top. Mound icing in center of cake top and spread it out to blend with the edges. Use plenty of icing, making sure cake is completely covered. Use long, even strokes.

Smooth top using a long metal ruler or piece of stiff cardboard. Pull straight across cake, bringing excess icing toward you. Smooth sides by holding a spatula against the side of the cake and slowly spinning the turntable or slowly turning the tray. When the icing sets, place cake on tray, cake board or assemble with other tiers.

Wilton Snow-white Buttercream

⅔ cup water
4 tablespoons meringue
powder
1¼ cups solid white
shortening
¾ teaspoon salt
¼ teaspoon butter flavoring
½ teaspoon almond flavoring
½ teaspoon clear vanilla
11½ cups sifted
confectioners' sugar

Combine water and meringue powder and whip at high speed until peaks form. Add four cups sugar, one cup at a time, beating after each addition at low speed. Alternately add shortening and remainder of sugar. Add salt and flavorings and beat at low speed until smooth. Thin with two teaspoons of white corn syrup per cup of icing for leaves and strings. Yields 8 cups. May be cut in half or doubled.

Wilton Classic Buttercream

⅓ cup butter
⅓ cup solid white shortening
1 teaspoon clear vanilla
⅛ teaspoon salt
1 pound confectioners' sugar,
sifted
5 tablespoons cool milk

Cream butter and shortening. Beat in sugar, 1 cup at a time, blending well after each addition and scraping sides and bottom of bowl with a spatula frequently. Add milk and beat at high speed until light and fluffy. Keep icing covered with lid or damp cloth and store in refrigerator. Bring to room temperature and rebeat to use again. Thin the same as Snow-white Buttercream. Yields 3 cups.

Wilton Boiled Icing

2 cups granulated sugar
½ cup water
¼ teaspoon cream of tartar
4 egg whites (room
temperature)
1½ cups sifted confectioners'
sugar

Boil granulated sugar, water, cream of tartar to 240°F. When boiling starts, brush sides of pan with warm water to prevent crystals forming. Brush again halfway through, but do not stir. Meanwhile, whip egg whites 7 minutes at high speed. Add boiled sugar mixture slowly, beat 3 minutes at high speed. Turn to second speed, gradually add confectioners' sugar, beat 7 minutes more at high speed Any grease will break down icing. Rebeating will not restore texture. Yields 3½ cups.

Wilton Royal Icing

3 egg whites (room
temperature)
1 pound confectioners' sugar
½ teaspoon cream of tartar

Combine ingredients and beat at high speed for 7 to 10 minutes. Very quick-drying, so keep covered at all times with damp cloth. Rebeating will not restore texture. Yields 3 cups.

This smooth, hard-drying icing is ideal for making flowers and other decorations in advance. After hardening, simply peel off wax paper and place, they never crumble! The perfect "cement" to attach decorations or fasten cake to plate. To make royal icing lighter, just whip it longer. Warning—the slightest bit of grease will break it down! Royal icing is *not* to be used for icing the cake.

Like every other work of architecture, a many-tiered wedding cake must start with a firm foundation. Hidden within the pounds of cake and icing is a framework of strong wooden dowel rods and plastic pegs—cleverly designed so it will not interfere with cutting or the number of servings.

Be sure to secure very large cakes to a strong serving plate or board, so that the final transporting will be easier and safer. The wedding cakes shown in this book were all iced and decorated in buttercream icing. (Boiled icing was used for cake on page 49.) Royal icing flowers were made in advance and attached when dry. Most tiers are two layers high with buttercream filling. Each is iced separately and supported as shown below.

HOW TO ASSEMBLE

A

WEDDING CAKE

1. Place the bottom tier of wedding cake on a base about 2 inches larger. Push a ¼" Wilton dowel rod into cake until it touches base. Then lift rod up, clip with pruning shear so it is level with top of cake and push back in again. Repeat until you have a circle of 7 dowel rods in bottom tier. (Use shear with one flat edge.)

2. Put a corrugated circle on top of bottom tier. (It should be wax-lined, so cake and icing will not soak into paper.) Then place next tier which is resting on its own corrugated circle into position. Insert five more dowel rods into this tier and clip level with top. To keep tiers from shifting, especially in warm weather, sharpen a long dowel rod at one end, tap through both bottom tiers, cut level with top.

3. The bottom of a Wilton tier separator has four plastic legs which snap into the separator's base plate. These add support and prevent slipping.

4. Before placing top tier in position on the separator's top plate, remove it from corrugated circle. (Otherwise it might slip.) You may decorate top tier on cake, but we suggest you take it off again for delivery and reassemble it at the reception. This will make for a safer delivery.

HOW TO DECORATE A WEDDING CAKE

The first thing to remember is that a wedding cake, as grand and as impressive as it may look, is just a series of regular cakes put together. The borders, flowers and decorations are ones you have done on smaller cakes—the familiar shell, rosette, star, leaf and rose appear again and again. If you know how to pipe as few as two borders, one flower, a leaf and a stem, you can turn out a fabulous wedding cake! And there is nothing to compare with the glow of pride you will feel when the compliments start coming your way!

Fill, ice and assemble your cake as described and you are ready to decorate! It is a good idea to make all flowers ahead of time and to have all trims, icing and equipment close at hand. Start at the bottom and work your way up. Keep the size of your borders uniform and the spaces between even. A neat, trim appearance will add much to the beauty and perfection of your cake. Use royal icing for "glue" to attach flowers and trim to the cake.

HOW TO TRANSPORT A WEDDING CAKE

Make sure it is on a large, strong base, at least 2" wider than the cake all around. Let it dry thoroughly after decorating (at least a half hour), then remove top tier or tiers to carry separately. (Replace them at the reception.) Carve a depression in a large 3" or 4" thick piece of soft foam so it is the exact size of the separator plate or base plate. Place the foam in the back of the car on a level surface—either in the back of a station wagon or on a platform made to level the back seat—and set the tiers in the depressions in the foam. Using this method a cake can be safely transported almost any distance.

To protect the cake from the sun or dust, carefully cover it with pieces of the very lightweight plastic bags used by dry cleaners. Anything heavier will crush icing or trim.

WEDDING CAKE CUTTING GUIDE

This serving chart for wedding cakes is based on 1" x 2" servings, two layers high. To cut any tiered cake, start by removing the top tier. Then begin cutting the second tier, third, and fourth. The count of servings includes the top tier, although many people remove this and freeze it for the first anniversary.

To cut a round tier, move in two inches from outer edge, cut a circle and cut 1" wide slices within it. Move in another two inches, cut another circle, and slice it into 1" pieces, continuing until each tier is cut. The center core of each tier and the small top tier can be cut into two, four, six or more pieces.

To cut square tiers, move in 2" from outer edge and cut straight across. Slice into 1" pieces. Move in another 2" and slice this section into 1" pieces. Continue until entire tier is cut.

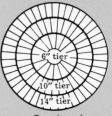

Top view of 3-tiered round cake.

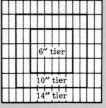

Top view of 3-tiered square cake.

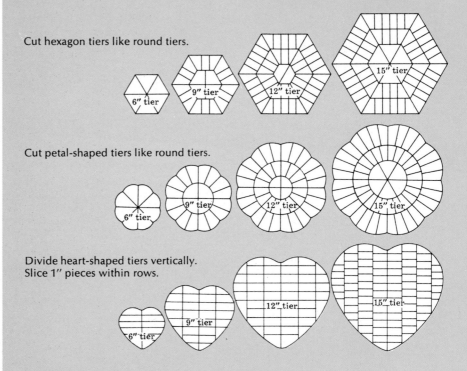

Cut hexagon tiers like round tiers.

Cut petal-shaped tiers like round tiers.

Divide heart-shaped tiers vertically. Slice 1" pieces within rows.

WEDDING CAKE SERVING CHART
Following the diagrams, here are the number of servings each tier provides.

SHAPE	SIZE	SERVINGS	SHAPE	SIZE	SERVINGS
ROUND	6"	16	HEXAGON	6"	6
	8"	30		9"	22
	10"	48		12"	50
	12"	68		15"	66
	14"	92			
	16"	118	PETAL	6"	8
	18"	148		9"	20
				12"	44
SQUARE	6"	18		15"	62
	8"	32			
	10"	50	HEART	6"	12
	12"	72		9"	28
	14"	98		12"	48
	16"	128		15"	90
	18"	162			

CENTERPIECE CAKES FOR

Anniversary Celebrations

A wedding anniversary is always worth celebrating, for it highlights a milestone in a happy married life. The designs that follow prove the anniversary cake can echo the pomp and prettiness of the original wedding masterpiece. Most, with a change in color and top ornament, can serve as wedding cake designs.

Anniversary parties for young marrieds can be informal and lots of fun, built around a theme of interests or traditions. But when twenty-five, forty or especially fifty years have passed, the anniversary party can be as formal as a wedding reception. (If you are arranging such a major celebration, you can follow the suggestions in Chapter II.)

TRADITIONAL ANNIVERSARY GIFTS
These are the kind of gifts tradition tells us to give on various wedding anniversaries. They can also provide a theme for your party or cake design.

YEAR	TYPE OF GIFT
First	Paper
Second	Cotton
Third	Leather
Fourth	Fruits, Flowers or Silk
Fifth	Wood
Sixth	Sugar, Candy or Iron
Seventh	Woolen or Copper
Eighth	Bronze or Pottery
Ninth	Willow or Pottery
Tenth	Tin or Aluminum
Eleventh	Steel
Twelfth	Silk or Linen
Fourteenth	Ivory
Fifteenth	Crystal
Twentieth	China
Twenty-Fifth	Silver
Thirtieth	Pearl
Thirty-Fifth	Coral
Fortieth	Ruby
Forty-Fifth	Sapphire
Fiftieth	Golden
Fifty-Fifth	Emerald
Sixtieth and Seventy-Fifth	Diamond

78

CELEBRATE GOLDEN YEARS
with our enchanting "Dream of Gold"
celebration cake. Tiny golden hearts and
flowers show up everywhere to set
the theme for your most important party in
half a century. Carry it out with more
golden hearts and flowers on napkins,
mints and cookies. Serves 216.

To make this golden cake: prepare an 8″ tier, place on 10″ separator and divide into eighths. Prepare a 12″ tier, place on a 14″ separator and divide into twelfths. Prepare a 16″ tier and divide into sixteenths. Assemble with tall Roman columns as shown. Make a large quantity of pale yellow drop flowers with tubes #225 and #190. Center with golden gel and set aside to dry. At top of all tiers (at each division mark) zigzag a heart design with tube #14. Pipe a small zigzag crescent from heart to heart. On 8″ and 16″ tier, use egg yellow gel and tube #1 to bead around each heart, over tops of crescents and to shape free-hand sprays. With same, pipe tiny graduated hearts on 12″ tier. At bottom of all tiers: pipe shell with tube #16 all around. Then use tube #18 to zigzag deep scallops under each heart with points meeting evenly beneath free-hand bead designs. Overpipe beading with tube #1. Attach drop flowers as shown. Pipe in leaves with tubes #65 and #67. For center of tiers: turn ornament base upside down. Attach drop flowers to florist wire and insert sprays. Use golden gel to bead on trim, following heart design on top and center ornaments.

A RUBY FOR 40

A jewel of a cake. Deep ruby touches gleam in medallions and trim. Echo the ruby garnet roses in the centerpieces for your tables. Serves 216.

How to make:
Prepare three tiers, 8", 12" and 16", glue bell in place and assemble as shown. Use Wilton template patterns for inner separator plate and side-of-cake designs. Trace patterns with pencil on plate and with toothpick on cake sides. With tube #13 and white icing, zigzag entire design on plate and cake sides, then over-pipe with red beads using tube #1 and piping gel. Do garland around top tier with tube #16, around center tier with tube #17 and around bottom tier with tube #18. Use tube #1 and red piping gel to do teardrops in between and for trim on bell, ornament and topmost vase. Use tube #3 to fill in "jewels". Set vase filled with fresh roses on top.

A ROSE-AND-RUFFLE CAKE TO MARK THE TWENTY-FIFTH

A celebration cake of Victorian lavishness! The lush beauty
of a summer garden is captured in the pink rose bouquets placed
at every turn and the pretty gazebo at the top. Serves 216.

How to decorate: prepare three tiers, 8″, 12″ and 16″ round
and assemble as shown. Frost in white buttercream and do
base borders of large puffs on all tiers with tube #199.
Overpipe each puff with a little pink ruffle, using tube
#101s, then add zigzag scallop at base with tube #14.
For top borders on all tiers first drop triple stringwork with
tube #2. Then repeat puff border as described above. Pipe
out large roses with tube #104 ahead of time and position
in clusters as shown. Finish off with artificial lily of the
valley, silver leaves. Between tiers: invert large and medium-
size sugar filigree bells on tulle. Insert lily of the valley,
put roses all around.

AN UNUSUAL "PETITS FOURS" CAKE TO CELEBRATE THE 50TH

An elegant new idea that's easy to make and easier to serve. The lavish party cake at top is just the right size for the table of honor—and the little white and gold petits fours below will delight everyone else. Make as many petits fours as you have guests.

How to decorate: prepare a two layer cake 10" round and frost in pale golden egg yellow buttercream. Do garlands, fleur de lis, top and bottom shell borders with tube #16 and large roses with tube #104. Place gold metallic leaves around roses and a gold metallic 50th anniversary medallion at top. For petits fours, make a large sheet cake and cut into diamond, square and round shapes about 2" long. Place on a rack and pour on white and gold-tinted fondant of any flavor. Top with small frosting roses made with tube #102 and leaves made with tube #67, anniversary emblems or trims such as the ring-and-doves shown.

ANNIVERSARY ORNAMENTS . . . THE CROWNING TOUCH!

Precious Years—certain to be a treasured keepsake when cake and celebration are just a memory. A frilly filigree heart serves as backdrop for the happy pair.

Brandy Snifter Keepsake—tiny couple and pair of lacy hearts are enshrined in crystal-clear glass. A beautiful tribute that will enhance the cake of cakes, serve forever as a memento.

50th Anniversary Wreath—a treasure in gold, meant to honor couples whose love has lasted for 50 wonderful years. Simple, but beautiful—a precious souvenir for the special pair.

82

A ROSE BALLET FOR 20 YEARS

A flowering, feminine look that brings to mind the
wondrous wedding cake of four decades past. Details
have the fine delicacy of porcelain, most
appropriate to a china anniversary. Serves 70.

How to Fashion:
Prepare a pair of two-layer cakes, 8" and 14" round and assemble as shown. Pipe scrolls on sides of bottom tier with
tube #16 and do top and bottom shell borders for this tier
with tube #19. Do garlands on top tier with tube #4, overpiping them with zig zag and tube #16 to make them stand
out. Put in stringwork to form lattice with tube #2, then
place a zigzag border at top for a neat look with tube #16.
Do the single garland at bottom of top tier with tube #16
again and drop two rows of stringwork over it with tube
#2. Do flowers ahead of time—roses with tube #101 and
#103 and Forget-Me-Nots with tube #101s—and place on
cake as shown. Pipe in small and large leaves where needed
with tubes no. 65 and 67. Place anniversary medallions as
shown.

HOW do I love thee? Let me count the ways.
I love thee to the depth and breadth and height
My soul can reach, when feeling out of sight
For the ends of Being and ideal Grace.
I love thee to the level of every day's
Most quiet need, by sun and candlelight.
I love thee freely, as men strive for Right;
I love thee purely, as men turn from Praise.
I love thee with the passion put to use
In my old griefs, and with my childhood's faith.
I love thee with a love I seemed to lose
With my lost saints—I love thee with the breath,
Smiles, tears, of all my life!—and, if God choose,
I shall but love thee better after death.
Elizabeth Barrett Browning

FESTOONS OF FLOWERS FOR THE 15TH

One of the prettiest little cakes that ever hailed a crystal anniversary! Serves 15.

How to fashion: pipe white sweet peas ahead with tube #102. Then use tube #4 to trace green vines all around a 10" two-layer cake. Attach sweet peas as shown, pipe in leaves with tube #66. Do curved guidelines for latticed sections with tube #16, string in latticework with tube #2. Use tube #14 to do curved zig zag border above lattice, tube #16 to overpipe it with scroll. Finish with tube #14 and another zig zag border for a neat edge. Pipe bottom garland-and-scroll borders with tube #16.

YELLOW ROSES FOR THE 10TH

The "tin" anniversary and the first really important celebration! Make the most of it with this truly romantic design. Serves 20.

How to fashion: prepare one 12" round two-or-three layer cake and frost in white buttercream. Pipe large and medium-size roses with tube #103 and #104 and rosebuds with tube #102 and dry thoroughly. Do bottom curved-shell border with tube #98 and top shell border with tube #16. Pipe vine on cake sides with tube #3 and leaves with tube #67. Mound some frosting on cake to indicate curve of garland and press roses into it as shown. Top with ornament.

87

A young, lively look for the "wooden" anniversary and so very easy to do! For heart pattern, fold wax paper in half, scratch in half of design with sharp pin. Cut out, trace on top of frosted 12-inch cake with toothpick. Zig zag around pattern with tube #14. Do drop flowers with tube #136, message with tube #2, top shell border with tube #19, bottom with tube #22. Serves 20.

A HAPPY HEART
FOR NUMBER FIVE

AND A PAPER NOSEGAY
FOR THE FIRST!

Bright way to celebrate their "paper" anniversary! Divide a 12-inch cake with dots and stringwork done with tube #3, then center these with flowers made with Wilton Color-Flow icing. (Do in two parts for curved effect—two petals, then three petals). Do flat ruffle border with tube #402, finish with a bouquet of paper flowers, Wilton sugar letters. Serves 20.

Parties BEFORE THE HAPPIEST DAY

There are so many pleasant ways to pay homage to the wedding couple—and we've shown just about all of them in this chapter. From announcement parties to bridal luncheons, bachelor and rehearsal dinners, all can be given a special flair!

One of the most familiar of before-wedding parties is the bridal shower. According to legend, the first shower took place in Holland when a young maiden who wanted to marry a poor miller, could not obtain her father's consent. This meant no dowry, a great drawback at the time. Friends came to the rescue and "showered" the bride with gifts so she could marry anyway.

Most showers are girls-only affairs, but lately, more and more showers are being given to which the men are also invited. These can be great fun, but gifts should be something both bride and groom can use. There are even showers for the groom these days — usually given by his ushers. Showers can happen any hour of the day — at brunch, luncheon, tea, cocktail time, dinner or after. And they are always informal.

The theme around which you plan the decorations, flowers, cake and other refreshments for your shower can come from the gifts to be given: personal, linen, kitchen, housekeeping, etc. for a girl shower—game room, bar, pantry, etc. for a couple shower. Or take your cue from other things, such as the couple's favorite sport or the way or place in which they met.

The ideas that follow may suit the parties you are planning—or at least, help get your own great ideas started!

MAKE EVERYTHING FESTIVE

with charming party accessories, such as the Wilton ones, shown at left. Use diminutive umbrellas and baskets to trim the cake (see page 97), or as nut and candy cups. Inscribe the mini-flower pots with the name of each guest for amusing place markers. Tie tiny shower cans to your gift package or use larger ones to hold candy. We've shown just a sampling of the dozens of favors Wilton offers and just a few of the ways you can use them. Your own imagination and ingenuity will invent many more!

ADD YOUR OWN SPECIAL TOUCHES

Do unusual things with cookies, mints and sugar cubes . . . to make every detail of your party look keyed to the occasion. Cut cookies into the bridal pair's initials or into heart shapes and trim with a dainty drop flower, made ahead with tube #225. Pipe in tiny leaves with tube #65, outline with tube #2. Use same tubes to pipe drop flowers and leaves on pastel mints and tiny sugar cubes. Pipe frosting hearts on mints with thinned royal icing and tube #3. (Make tinted flower and heart-shaped sugar cubes with Wilton sugar molds.)

THE PARENTS OF THE BRIDE GIVE AN ELEGANT DINNER

Honored guests are the parents of the groom. As a special treat, a luxurious Hasselnusstorte (Hazelnut Cake) graces the table. The three-layer torte is made from the traditional hazelnut cake recipe and filled with raspberry jam. **Decorate in the Viennese manner:** frost with sweetened whipped cream and pipe mocha buttercream lines and rosettes with tube #30. Top with toasted hazelnuts and center with a circle of raspberry jam.

THE GOOD NEWS IS TOLD AT AN INTIMATE TEA

Such a charming idea! On the occasion when you break the news, use your nicest serving pieces to present such appealing tidbits as flower-topped petits fours, tiny cream-filled cornucopias and rich butter cookies. **To make petits fours:** bake a sponge cake in a jelly roll pan. Cut in half (it will handle more easily, if baked a day or two ahead) and fill the layers with jam or butter cream. Brush top with hot apricot glaze and trim all crisp edges. Cut with a sharp knife (wiping frequently) into squares or diamonds. Place cakes on a wire rack so melted fondant can be poured over, icing all sides. Trim with pre-made flowers.

SAY OLÉ WITH A GAY MEXICAN FIESTA!

Start with our colorful Spanish-look chrysanthemum cake at left. Add spicy refreshments of tacos and enchiladas. **To make:** assemble 10" and 14" square tiers as shown. Make ahead—filigree design (see Wilton pattern) with tube #1, overpiping for strength. Do flowers with tube #81 and leaves with tube #4. Attach filigree with wet icing. Pipe double bead borders with tube #5. Attach flowers and leaves last.

THE BRIDESMAIDS GIVE THE FIRST SHOWER

And they cheer the bride with a cake that's knee-deep in field flowers! **To make:** do all borders with tube #18. First pipe zig-zag bottom border, then do top border as follows: press out garland, fill with a crescent, overpipe with zig-zag scallop. Pipe cornflowers with tube #14, daisies with tube #103, wild roses with tube #101 and leaves with tube #67. Do umbrella flowers with tube #101s, leaves with tube #67s, beading with tube #1.

Idea: put small gifts for the bride in a Mexican pinata!

THE BRIDE GIVES A LUNCHEON FOR HER BRIDESMAIDS

And perhaps, observes a charming old custom by baking a trinket into the cake. The girl who finds it, marries next! **To fashion cake:** frost a two-layer cake 10" square and pipe big reverse shells for bottom border, regular shells for top border with tube #32. Do side scrolls with tube #14, overpipe with circular "e" motion. Pipe roses, ribbon bow with tube #104, stem with #2, daisies with #103, forget-me-nots with #101s.

. . . AND PRESENTS EACH WITH A GIFT

The small, but thoughtfully-chosen gifts a bride gives her attendants—pearls, bracelets, charms—fit beautifully into these enchanting little covered gift boxes with the look of engraved antique silver. The heart-shaped box, embelished with scrolls and cupids, is a faithful replica of a precious silver heirloom. And the beflowered cup has windows to allow a peep inside. They'll hold trinkets later—or tiny straw flower bouquets . . . or nuts and mints at a party.

SHOWERS ARE FOR FUN . . . AND LOTS OF GIRLISH GOSSIP

So give the bride gay daisy bouquets on a cake that's sure to start the conversation going! Petite parasols double as nut and candy cups. **To make:** frost a two-layer cake 10″ round in buttercream. Pipe bottom shell border with tube #20—reverse shell border with tube #18. Make daisies ahead of time with tubes #102 and #103. Do yellow centers with tube #4 and leaves with tube #66 and attach to wires. Add ribbon bows.

Springtime

SHOWER A SPRING BRIDE
Wish her joy that blooms forever with our spring garden cake! **To fashion:** frost 14" square cake and pipe bottom shell border with tube #4B, top reverse shell with tube #20. Do flowers ahead: larkspur (on wires) and Forget-Me-Nots with tube #101s, daffodils, daisies with tube #102, #103. Leaves, #67. Add miniature watering can and garden fence to complete the pretty picture.

FETE A SUMMER BRIDE
Wish her a life filled with flowers via our gazebo garden cake. **To fashion:** frost a 10" round two-layer cake as shown. Make flowers ahead with tube #103 and #104, flower centers, top bead borders and stringwork with tube #4, bottom ribbon border with tube #104 and leaves with tube #66 and #65. Fill the little "urn" with icing fern leaves piped on to wires with tube #4.

Summertime

Snowtime

ARE THEY PLANNING A SKI HONEYMOON?

Then plan their shower or party cake around their favorite sport! **To fashion:** frost a two-layer cake 10", 11", or 12" square, with white buttercream. Swirl mounds of frosting on top to resemble snow and pipe a stand-up ribbon border at base with tube #0Z-402. Stand skis on top, tie with ribbons strung with "wedding rings" and place a pair of tiny plastic ski boots and ski poles at side.

$\mathscr{A}\ toast$ TO THE BRIDE-TO-BE

A SWEETER BOUQUET than the one she'll carry down the aisle on her day-of-days; **To fashion:** use one box of mix to bake a cake in a Wonder Mold pan, heap frosting all over. Attach lots of large and small white roses made ahead with tubes #102, #103 and #104. Pipe in leaves with tubes #66 and #70. Do tiny blue Forget-Me-Nots ahead with tube #101s, attach to wires with a bit of icing, then place as shown. Tuck a satiny bow at side.

DAISIES FOR THE GIRL WHO MARRIES IN MAY

Or any other month in spring! And they're showered on a cake that
looks for all the world like a sunshiny garden. Deck the table with fresh daisies
to pick up the pretty theme. And repeat colors in your tablecloth
and napkins. The perfect feminine touch for a trousseau or linen shower!

To make daisy cake: bake a two-layer cake, 8" square,
fill and frost all over with pale yellow buttercream icing.
Make daisies ahead of time in three sizes with tubes
#101s, 102 and #104 and dry thoroughly before placing
as shown. (Pipe a guideline for the garlands with green
icing and tube #4 before you attach the flowers.) Pipe
in leaves with tube #67. Do top reverse shell borders
and bottom large shell borders with tube #30. Place
daisy-filled cherub fountain at top.

To make violet cake: bake a two-layer cake 10" round.
Fill and frost with pale, cool green buttercream icing.
Pipe a white shell border at bottom and a zig zag scallop
over it with tube #16. Pipe another zig zag over that
with tube #14. Pipe a white triple shell border at top
with tube #14. Do violets ahead of time with tube #59
and leaves with tube #102. Dry both violets and leaves
thoroughly before placing as shown all around bottom
border and in bouquet at top. Add a real ribbon bow.

A VIOLET NOSEGAY FOR THE APRIL BRIDE

On a pretty cake that sets the scene with fresh spring colors! For linen
shower gifts, cover a cardboard "hope" chest with green crepe paper ruffles.
Pin little violet bouquets here and there on it. For a lingerie shower,
cover a carton to look like a dressing table.

GIVE AN ELEGANT CHAMPAGNE PICNIC ON THE GRASS

It may seem like pure magic to your guests, but it takes less effort than you may think to
transform the traditional care-free picnic into a shower or pre-wedding party worthy of the
Arabian Nights. Put your finest china and serving pieces in a sylvan setting and accompany such delicacies
as Beef Wellington slices or pate-stuffed chicken breasts with chilled champagne. Then,
taking a cue from nature, serve colorful, flower cup-cakes as a final sweet.

GATHER THE GIRLS FOR COFFEE, CAKE AND TALK

And make yours a dessert shower—easy for you and relaxing fun for everyone who attends! Center your table with blossom-decked wedding bell cakes and pick up the spring colors in tablecloth, napkins and flowers. Then all you have to add is coffee or tea and perhaps ice cream in bell-shaped molds. Wrap and ribbon the gifts in colors to match the cake, and heap them on a card table covered with a gay cloth.

To make flower cupcakes: take simple cupcakes, hold in your left hand like a flower nail and, turning as you go, pipe flowers right on top with large flower tubes. You can do the daisy and the carnation with tube #124—both kinds of roses and the jonquils with tube #127. Do the lovely chrysanthemum with tube #79. Pipe in leaves with large leaf tube #68. Pipe the shell and zig zag borders with tube #14 and be sure to do them before you start piping flowers!

To make wedding bell cakes: bake two cakes in bell-shaped pans and frost white. Use tube #4 for gold beading outline and stripes, and for triple bead border at bottom. Do bead outline for mouth of bells with tube #6. Pipe flowers in advance, using tube #104 for poppies, wild flowers, large daisies and sweet peas. Use #102 for medium daisies and smaller flowers, 101s for forget-me-nots. Attach as shown, pipe in leaves with tube #67.

EVERY PROSPECTIVE GROOM IS ENTITLED TO HIS JUST DESSERTS

More and more groom's showers are now being given and during such important "launching" ceremonies the climate in which the strictly masculine guests gather should be relaxed. For a worthy centerpiece, serve a rich devil's food cake, frosted in mocha-flavored buttercream.

THE BACHELOR DINNER—FAREWELL TO SINGLE DAYS

The groom gathers his friends and ushers for the traditional males-only dinner. The menu features foods than men like best—and the star of the feast is the dessert, a delicious rum-soaked cake flourished with whipped cream and filled with a rich custard. The original *Zuppa Inglese* was created in Italy but appeals to everyone, especially men.

To make groom's cake at left: bake a two-layer devil's food cake, 10" round. Cool, fill with creamy white filling and frost with mocha buttercream at sides, white on top. Pipe bottom shell border with tube #4B, top shell border with tube #32. Cut chocolate wafers in half and place between each bottom shell. Write the merry message with tube #2 and use the Wilton coach, horses and tiny groom for trim.

To make the Zuppa Inglese: bake a sponge cake in a loaf pan, 4½" x 9". When cool, split into 3 layers and sprinkle layers with a cup of rum. Spread almond-flavored custard between the layers. Refrigerate for several hours. Just before serving, fill a pastry bag with sweetened, vanilla-flavored whipped cream and with tube #2E, pipe scrolls and swirls as shown. For a final colorful flourish, decorate with candied violets.

107

SWEET TOUCHES FOR YOUR SHOWER...

Add charm to gift packages and party tables with trims and trinkets such as
these from Wilton . . . satiny artificial roses and lily of the valley,
porcelain-look plastic angels and serene swans. The tiny parasols are decked
with colorful drop flowers . . . all piped with tube #224.

How to decorate Rehearsal Dinner cake: assemble three tiers, one 6″, another 12″ and a third tiny tier, 2½″ round. Frost all with shocking pink buttercream. For bottom tier, pipe pink shell border at base with tube #32 and ribbon border at top with tube #104. Fill ribbon with zig zag, drape stringwork with tube #4 and finish off with ribbon bows. For middle tier, pipe white shell border at bottom with tube #16 and standing shell borders at top with tube #22, drop stringwork with tube #4. For tiny top tier, do top shells with tube #16, bottom ones with tube #14. Make roses ahead with tube #102 and position after drying, using artificial stems and leaves and a real ribbon bow for bride's bouquet effect. Push Wilton stairway into place and position bride and groom and attendant dolls as shown.

The Rehearsal Dinner...

THE GROOM'S FAMILY ENTERTAINS THE
WEDDING PARTY WITH A CENTERPIECE
PRETTY AS THE WEDDING CAKE

WILL THEY HONEYMOON ON A TROPICAL ISLE?

Then salute the happiness ahead with a flamboyant orchid cake. And serve luau style—with everyone seated on cushions around a "table" made of mats. Have luscious island tidbits—chicken pineapple, fried rice, broiled shrimp, coconut fruit salad and tropical punch.

How to make an Orchid Cake: frost a two-layer cake 12 inches round in pale green buttercream. Fashion an orchid of gum paste or use a real one! Make top and bottom border with our multi-coupler that does two or three borders at one time. (For top border, use tube #104 on top, #30 in center and #104 at bottom of coupler. For base border, use two tubes, #30 and #104 in coupler.) Do side string borders with regular pastry bag and tube #3. Gather tulle into a pouff and fasten with a few stitches. Then fasten orchid to pouff and place as shown at top of cake.

SHOWER THE BRIDE WITH COOKBOOKS

Breathes there a bride who couldn't use a little help around the
kitchen? She'll be grateful for your cookbooks over and over later on and so
will her new husband! Complete the party fun with a book cake,
brightly beflowered and appropriately inscribed.

How to make a bridal Book Cake: bake a cake in two book-shaped pans, filling
both with single box of cake mix batter. (Grease and flour before pouring in batter.) Bake according to package directions, then unmold carefully on wax paper
and cool. Place cakes together on a cardboard base and frost all over. Use decorating comb or table fork to do "pages" on sides. Pipe tiny scroll page borders,
letters and heart with tube #3. Do flowers with tube #104, dry thoroughly and
place as shown. Pipe in leaves with tube #67.

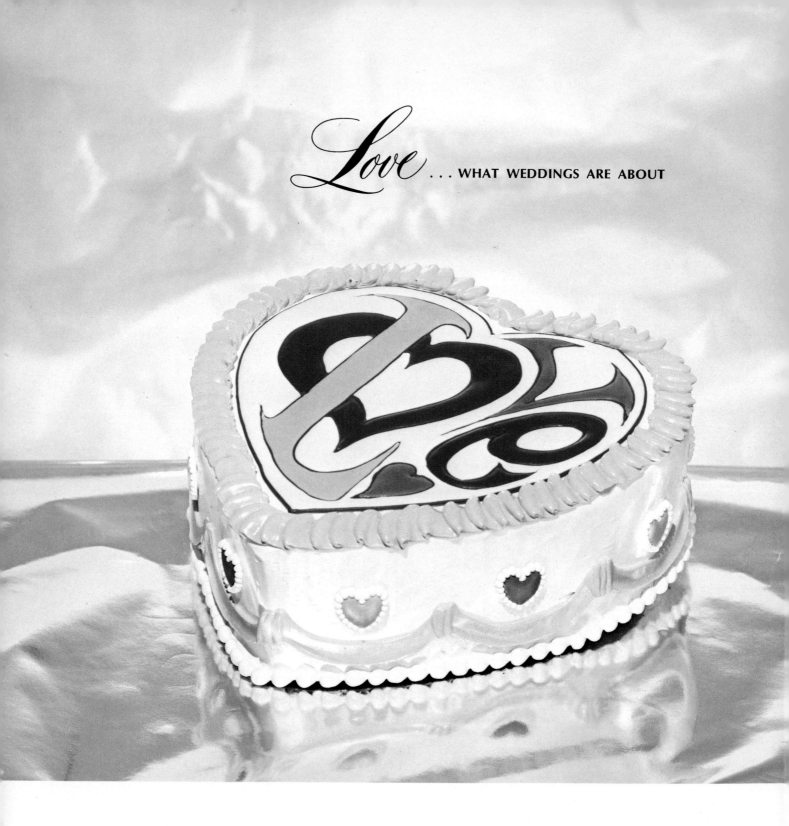

And it's all spelled out for you on this sweet, mod cake that will add excitement to a bridal shower or any before-the-wedding party. The bright monochromatic color scheme, the hearts chasing each other around the sides, the gleaming ribbon borders give a festive flair!

HOW TO MAKE A "LOVE" CAKE. Bake a cake in a heart-shaped pan. Then tape Wilton Love pattern to a piece of cardboard, cover with wax paper, cellophane or saran—wrapping tightly to remove all wrinkles. Outline design with stiffened Color Flow icing and small tube #1 or #2. Thin icing with a few drops of water so it will "flow" and press out gently inside outline. Finally fill in center and dry at least 48 hours before peeling off to place on frosted cake. Do side hearts same way. Use tube #104 to pipe top ribbon and side swag border. Pipe bead heart outline and bottom dot borders with tube #3.